The Gentle Giant

by Lynn Marr-Moore

assisted by
Dr. Harold Nichols

Library of Congress Control Number: 2001089551
ISBN Number: 1-888223-21-9

The Gentle Giant

Chris Taylor
1950-1979

The Gentle Giant

FOREWARD

Throughout the course of a person's lifetime, there are individuals who touch your life and touch it deeply. As a childhood friend, fellow student and athlete, but more importantly, as a best friend as I grew through the high school to young adult years, Chris Taylor was one of those individuals in my life. To lose such a person at the early age of twenty-nine is both testing and shattering. It can be understood best only by someone who has experienced such an untimely loss. What may be even more frustrating is the fear that the qualities and abilities that were joined together in that very special individual may be lost forever.

In a relatively short lifetime, Chris Taylor attained state, national and international recognition as a superior amateur wrestler. He was a rare combination of gentleness and extraordinary strength, massive size yet deceptive quickness, and fierce competitiveness with off-the-mat compassion, especially for the very young. He overcame what seemed like an endless stream of obstacles throughout his life, by using the gifts many thought of as burdens. His combination of hard work and dedication brought him from a joked about fat boy to an international hero. It allowed him to accomplish more in a short time than most can attain in a much longer lifetime.

The story of Chris Taylor's life can serve as an inspiration for any young athlete from the very gifted to the slower excellor. It is motivational material for any parent or coach to teach their young athletes the rewards of hard work and dedication, as well as humility with success. It is with a great deal of confidence that I thank the book's sponsor, Dr. Harold Nichols, and its author, Lynn Marr-Moore, for their intense effort to tell Chris's story as factually as humanly possible. Through their efforts, I hope you will come to know a man I loved as a brother and miss deeply as a friend. His life story is an outstanding example of courage for competitors of all ages.

Dr. Charles Burling
Dowagiac, Michigan

Introduction

It was many years ago when Dr. Harold Nichols approached me to come to work for him. He had recently retired, after coaching 35 years at Iowa State University and was on a mission. I tried to convince him that I already had a job. He in turn tried to convince me that I should help him with several projects. I soon learned that it was very difficult, if not impossible, to tell Dr. Nichols "no".

My no soon turned to a yes. I have always been a firm believer in the concept that something good comes out of everything. Sometimes it just takes a little longer for the good to surface. Not too much time had passed, before the "good" came to light.

Dr. Nichols, soon known to me as "Nick", did have several projects for me. He walked up to me one day in the office in Ames and pointed to the wall poster of Chris Taylor holding Hilton Coliseum over his head. Chris wrestled for Nick at ISU and eventually was a competitor in one of the most talked about Olympic wrestling matches in history. He lived a hard, short life, dying very tragically at the young age of 29 leaving his wife and daughter behind. Nick said to me very matter of fact: "Yes, someone needs to tell the story of *The Gentle Giant*, and I want you to do it for me Lynn."

I was just a little taken aback by the enormous project. Quite literally, Chris was an enormous man, and this truly would be an enormous project. After all, Chris wasn't even alive to help me. I attacked it with my heart and soul. Never having met Chris, I didn't know where to begin this journey. I threw myself into the project with my total being and along the way, I met Chris Taylor, the little boy, the young man, the son and brother, the athlete, the husband and the father. Through my research on Chris I had the pleasure of meeting his wife, parents, sisters, friends and his numerous fans around the world.

I spent several years writing, researching and re-writing the Chris Taylor story. Dr. Nichols allowed me to do whatever I needed and supported me along the way. Chris's family and friends were always available when I had questions, and his many teammates from Iowa State supplied numerous stories to fill this book.

Chris was truly a "Gentle Giant". He was a giant of a man, living in a small person's world. At one point in my writing I felt that I had to stop. I was dealing with Chris's death. I simply walked away. I thought to myself that I just couldn't do this. Then, one night, I went to my office and I wrote all night long. I had the feeling that someone was watching me. I would turn to see if it was one of my sons, but no one would be there. The next morning I called Chuck Burling in Michigan and told him about my experience. He commented that he had no doubt that it was Chris watching over my shoulder. He probably wanted to make sure that I had gotten the final chapter in his life story correct. And, it had been the anniversary of his death.

Many people are responsible for this book finally happening. You all know who you are. Special thank you's are also in order:

- In Memory of my father, Charles W. Marr, whom I miss so much and who encouraged me every step of the way. He instilled in me the concept of running my own race. I wish he were alive to see this project in final form.
- To my sons, Timmothy, Ted and Travis, who all did their time on "the Mat" and taught me so much about a wrestler's life.
- To Lynn, Chris's wife, for the endless contributions of her time with Chris.
- To my dear friend Chuck Burling, who was my right-hand-man throughout this entire project. Without your help, Chuck, this never would have happened.
- To Mike Chapman, for his direction and words.
- To Dan Gable for his kind words.
- To my Publisher, Ron McMillen, who has always believed in me and the Chris Taylor story.
- To Dave Popelka, my designer, who made my words come to life on paper.
- To my husband, Reed, who so kindly and with perfection went through this story, one word at a time. No one else could have done a better job.
- And finally, to one of my dearest friends, Dr. Harold Nichols, in whose memory, I dedicate this work.

The Chris Taylor story is a true story which will inspire everyone who reads it. It is not just the story of a wrestler, but it is the story of a remarkable life.

Read, laugh, cry, enjoy and most of all, make a new friend in Chris Taylor, *The Gentle Giant*.

Lynn Marr-Moore

The Author, at right, with Dr. Harold Nichols (Nick).

The Gentle Giant

Dr. Harold Nichols

Dr. Harold Nichols was a soft-spoken man with a winning attitude. A humble man, a man of few words, he didn't have to say much to get his point across not only in the world of business, but also to his wrestlers. As one reporter so eloquently said at the time of his death, "He was a man of few words, and when he spoke, people listened."

Dr. Nichols was Iowa State Wrestling for 35 years. He was the man at the helm and has been considered one of the most successful coaches of all time. During his time as head coach at Iowa State, his teams completed a dual meet record of 456-75-11. He was coach to 38 NCAA Champions, 91 Big Eight Champions and seven Olympians. His teams accomplished an amazing six national team titles. More affectionately known as "Nick", he too was considered a champion of his time, being named National Coach of the Year four times. In recognition of his profound influence on the lives of his wrestlers as a coach, teacher and friend, Dr. Nichols was honored as a Distinguished Member of the National Wrestling Hall of Fame. His accolades go on and on.

One of the Olympians was none other than Chris Taylor. Nick was particularly fond of the "Gentle Giant" from Dowagiac, Michigan, who eventually came to wrestle at Iowa State. It wasn't until after Taylor's death and after Nick's retirement, that the Chris Taylor story was told. Due to the support, efforts and direction of Dr. Harold Nichols, this book was made possible.

Dr. Harold Nichols died in Ames, Iowa, at the age of 79 on February 22, 1997. He had suffered a stroke several years prior to his death.

The Author

The Gentle Giant

Table of Contents

Chris at the 1972 Olympics.

The Gentle Giant

CHAPTER 1
A Big Man Accepted by Small Men

Tbilisi is wrestling country. Perhaps no place in the world is the sport more appreciated, and its practitioners more revered. The city, located deep in the heart of the province of Georgia, in the southern portion of what use to be the Soviet Union, has seen wrestlers come and go for over a thousand years. Founded as part of the Persian Empire in the fourth century, Tbilisi has since been ruled by Mongols, Iranians, Turks, Moslems, Arabs and Khazar.

Currently an industrial center of some 700,000 citizens, Tbilisi has developed into an important component of what was known as the Soviet Union's economic structure. It has also become home to the world's most prestigious wrestling tournament. For nearly three decades, the globe's greatest amateur wrestlers have made the annual trek to Tbilisi, daring to test themselves against the very best the sport has to offer. The Soviet Union has dominated the international wrestling scene for the past thirty or so years and as the host country, enters as many as ten wrestlers in each of the ten weight classes. In order for a foreign wrestler to win a gold medal at Tbilisi, he must not only defeat the other foreign entries, but he must conquer several Russians...a factor that is missing at the world tournament or the Olympics, where each country is limited to a single entry.

The United States made its first appearance at a Tbilisi tournament in 1971. The only American winner that year was the talented Don Behm, a Michigan State University graduate who captured the 125.5 pound crown.

Dan Gable finished second at 149.5 pounds when he lost a 3-2 decision on a very controversial call. The following year he breezed through the tournament in such impressive style that the Soviet national coach, at the awards banquet following the competition, announced his number one goal for the 1972 Olympic Games in Munich was to find a Soviet wrestler who could defeat Gable.

But the main attraction of the 1971 Tbilisi tournament wasn't either Behm or Gable; both were swallowed up by the immense shadow of a giant from Michigan. The impact Chris Taylor made on the Soviet crowd was as overwhelming as the man himself, and offered an indication of something more important of things to come.

"I roomed with Chris on that Tbilisi trip in 1971, I'll never forget it," related Gable in the summer of 1988, seventeen years after the fact. "That's where I really got to know him for the first time."

Gable, sitting in his plush offices at the University of Iowa, leaned forward in his chair, relishing the opportunity to relive the moment.

"Back then, few wrestling teams warmed up in front of the crowd on the mats like we did. The Soviets never did. But the American team walked out in front of the crowd and began to warm up. There were maybe seven or eight thousand people there. Very knowledgeable fans.

"When we walked out onto the mats, you could hear a ripple of noise go through the crowd. They were all looking at Chris." He paused.

"The American team began warming up, slowly. But Chris just stood there, his arms folded across his chest. Then, he swung his arms out in front of him once, shortly.

"The crowd went crazy. They shouted and yelled and whistled. They loved it.

"We continued warming up, watching Chris and the crowd. He was just standing there. Then, he swung his arms a second time — and the crowd erupted again."

A smile crept across Gable's face, chiseled through thousands of hours of punishing workouts. He sagged back in his chair, caressing the scene as it played out in his mind.

"It grew quiet again. Chris continued to stand there. Then, suddenly, he did a forward somersault...and the whole place went up for grabs. The Soviets just went wild!"

Gable grinned again, shaking his head slowly at the memory.

"The Soviet security people had to come up and ask Chris to go behind the stands and finish warming up. The Soviets had never seen anything like him. His mere presence was causing a huge distraction."

Of course, causing a big distraction was not unusual for Chris Taylor. From his early years in Dowagiac, Michigan, when his parents took him to the University of Michigan to have him tested for his abnormal size, up through his high school career, to his collegiate days at Iowa State University, through the 1972 Olympics in Munich and the professional wrestling hot spots around the country, to his sad ending in Story City, Iowa, in 1979, the presence of Chris Taylor was an event. His presence alone was tantamount to a sideshow, apt to cause a bevy of stares at the least and near pandemonium at the most.

For while Chris Taylor does not meet all the criteria for being a giant, he came as close as any person most of us were ever likely to meet. According to Sarah Teale, author of the book "Giants": Anthropologists and medical specialists define a giant as being a person who stands over one foot, three inches taller than the average member of his society."

At a mere six foot five inches tall, Taylor did not meet that criterion. But Webster's dictionary defines a giant as "a person of unusual stature or size"; there is no doubt Chris Taylor met that definition head on.

Weighing in at over 440 pounds while in college and reportedly going over the 500 pound mark later on, Taylor belonged to a most unique category of the human species. By just about anyone's definition, he WAS a giant; not the terrifying type Jack found after climbing to the top of the beanstalk, but very intimidating nonetheless. A man of prodigious appetites in many respects, he was friendly and amiable the majority of the time. If children cowered under blankets during the telling of s they clamored to be near the wrestler who became known as the Gentle Giant.

And he welcomed them, one and all. It is indisputable that he spent far more time with fans after his match signing autographs than he did on the mat in actual competition.

"When Chris Taylor competes at a regular season dual meet nowadays it sometimes takes him 45 minutes to leave the arena," wrote Gordy Holt, a Seattle sportswriter, in 1972.

"It's the kids. They swarm around him, shoving pencils and paper toward his huge frame, touching and gawking."

In a society where "more" is often perceived as "better" Taylor was simply too large to always be on the receiving end of good intentions. In a world which yearns to make heroes of men who surpass others in stature, he was once unfairly penalized, because of his size, in a match which would become the most controversial in Olympic wrestling history.

Chris Taylor lived a life of paradoxes. He was unable to hide from himself, yet was constantly on display wherever and whenever he went. At the 1972 Olympics in Munich, he became a prisoner in the Olympic Village, stealing away at night in an attempt to avoid autograph seekers and those who hoped to see him in the flesh, up close and personal.

"Even the other athletes wouldn't leave him alone; they wanted their pictures taken with him," said Gable. "People just tried to get around him."

Taylor was often the object of great affection; at other times, great rudeness. While many admired the skill that he developed to

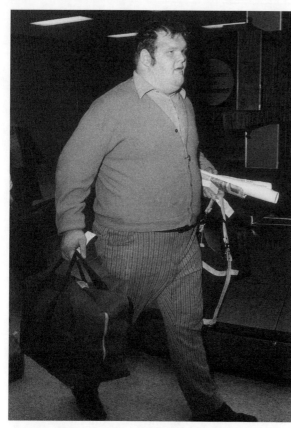

complement his incredible size, others gave him little credit, unable to comprehend the complex web of genetics, circumstances and events that had shaped him, both outwardly and internally.

"He was such a gentle guy, because his parents drove that into him," said Ed Huffman, one of his closest friends. Tipping the scales to near the 400 pound mark himself, Huffman is a man who understands what it is to be looked upon with a nervous smile. "Chris was always afraid of hurting someone; if Chris hadn't carried that fear around with him all his life, he would have been absolutely unbeatable, the greatest heavyweight wrestler who ever lived."

As it was, Taylor fans can stake a claim that he was the single most awesome force in the history of amateur wrestling, on or off the mat. Everywhere he went, he attracted stares and crowds. While the incomparable Gable could move through an airline terminal in virtual anonymity, Taylor was instantly recognizable.

"I could always spot our wrestling team whenever I went into an airport," remembered Dr. Harold Nichols, Taylor's coach at Iowa State University. "All I had to do was look for Chris. With his size, he could never hide."

But there was more than just the outward appearance. He was sensitive about his dimensions, even if he hid his feelings from all but his closest friends and at times he wished to be less than he was, at least physically.

"I don't mind being a giant," Taylor told writer Herman Weiskopf in a 1971 *Sports Illustrated* article, "but sometimes I'd like to be 190 pounds, or 105, to see what it would feel like. And I'd like to not always have to prove myself."

It was a poignant point made by a man

Photo courtesy of the Des Moines Register.

The Des Moines airport March 12,1972.

perhaps grown a bit weary with being what he was. "Most giants tried to be accepted and liked by small men," continued Sarah Teale. "Basically, they were friendly by nature and loved companionship, but they were easily hurt by rejection." Though she was writing primarily about imaginary giants in a land which never existed, her words ring true for modern giants who find themselves out of step with the society around them.

Yet, there were those who recognized Taylor was indeed more than he appeared to be.

"What people don't realize is how interesting a person he really was," said Gable. "He was a jovial guy, with a good sense of humor. And he could sing. I mean, really sing good. I will never forget him singing *Proud Mary*. It was good enough that he could have recorded it."

The life story of Chris Taylor, the gentle giant, is also one that should be recorded. Like the hero of the movie *Mask*, Taylor moved through life in a manner only a very tiny percentage of us will ever be able to comprehend to any degree. That he was able to do so with style and with grace is all the more to his credit.

Chris at about the age of 3.

Chris about ready to make a high school pin.

Chris and Ben Peterson at Cornorton's Camp.

CHAPTER 2
Chris Taylor - The "Little" Boy

Chris James Taylor entered the world on June 13, 1950, in Dowagiac, Michigan. He was the first of three children born to Vera McFee Taylor and James Taylor. It was an inauspicious debut for a man destined to be called a giant, as he tipped the scales at a mere seven and one-quarter pounds.

Vera had been born in Canada and moved to Dowagiac at the age of one and one-half, while Jim grew up in Decatar, Michigan. Vera worked as a bookkeeper at a dairy when they met, with Jim working as a meat cutter. The two were introduced by

Chris at 6 months.

friends and were married on September 17, 1949. After a move to Dowagiac, Jim found work as a trouble shooter for Michigan Power Company and Vera began working for General Telephone Company.

Dowagiac is a thriving community with a population of 6,300 located in Cass County, Michigan, in the southwest corner of the state, some fifty miles northeast of South Bend, Indiana.

The name Dowagiac came from a Potawatomi Indian word, Nodwagayuk, translated meaning

Chris at 1 year old.

"the foraging ground". The area abundantly supplied the need for wild game, fruits, vegetables, grains and medicinal herbs. The fields were surrounded by mammoth oak trees, hazel brush and other kinds of woods. Marvelous works could be found, left from the early Potawatomi Indians who once lived and farmed the land. Indian arrowheads made of pure quartz can still be found if one looks through the cornfields of present time.

There was no Chief Dowagiac, contrary to rumors. The name was incorporated in an advertising logo used by the round Oak Stove

Chris at 3 years old in Michigan.

Company located in Dowagiac. But a chief by the name of Chief Simon Pokagon from the Potawatomi Indian tribe was in Dowagiac at the time the settlers arrived.

Judge H.B. Tuthill spoke of Dowagiac back in 1932. His family had come to Dowagiac in 1854 and the family has a street named after them by the name of Cyrus Tuthill.

"Perhaps it is well known that the area of old Dowagiac within the confines of Silver Creek, was laid out by Patrick Hamilton. Originally it was part of his farm," said Tuthill.

Tuthill Street is so named for Cyrus Tuthill. Many of the settlers in Dowagiac and the vicinity came from the east and New York as well as from New England. They brought with them a keen desire to succeed and a love of the land. Both qualities were to influence the emotional development of the young boy who would someday make Dowagiac famous as the home of a gentle giant.

There were ancestors on Jim's side of the family who were large framed, but Vera's side of the family is much smaller. Chris's sisters Sherrie, born in 1955, and Becky, born in 1958, could almost be described as petite. Yet, Chris began growing at a rapid rate. His size, especially as a young child, became a concern to his parents...a concern that grew almost as rapidly as Chris himself.

"At six months Chris was good sized," said Vera in 1988, reflecting back nearly three decades. "When he was just five years old he weighed 75 pounds. We took him to Ann Arbor to have tests run on him at the University of Michigan Medical Center."

Two trips to the medical center failed to explain the accelerated growth pattern Chris was experiencing. The doctors could only add that Chris was bigger than the normal child — and added the unsettling fact that his heart was twice the size of the heart in a normal-sized child his age.

More was expected from Chris, being big all his life and especially as a child. But Chris was a happy child with all the frustrations which could have left him a very unhappy child. He learned at a young age to shrug off many of those frustrations and go about his business.

Chris's size as a child, abnormal as it was, did not limit his activities. He spent endless hours on his bike, roller skating and chasing his sisters in harmless games and activities. As he grew, he loved to go hunting and fishing with his dad and friends.

Chris had many friends and spent a lot of time in the family's back yard playing cowboy. He would take on the image of Roy Rogers and then turn to being Davy Crockett, complete with his

The Gentle Giant

coonskin cap or cowboy hat, whatever would be appropriate at the given time. His mother recalls him as the type of child who would not sit in the house and ponder what to do. He was always a busy child...and a gregarious one. He had a genuine interest in people that he carried with him throughout his entire life.

The Taylor family lived on Second Avenue in Dowagiac. "I would send Chris to the store and it would always take him half-an-hour to go those four blocks because he was a real talker and he would stop to visit with everyone in the neighborhood," said Vera. "He was very thoughtful and always wanted to help someone out," she added.

Chris learned to ride his bike at a very young age. He had a 14 inch two wheeler from which he couldn't quite reach the ground. He would start out at the board fence in front of his house where his grandfather had made a wooden box for him to get off and on. He would be on his bike and then take off across the street to where his grandparents lived. Chris went through several bikes in those years, all before he was even in school. But Jim and Vera kept buying the extra-heavy duty model in hopes they would last just a bit longer than the regular-sized model. Vera said he always enjoyed tearing around the neighborhood on his bike. His landing procedure consisted of simply crashing to come to a stop. The kids he ran with would even go to the playground at the nearby school and ride around it for hours, until the older kids forced them to leave.

"We lived across the street from Chris when he was growing up," said Marie McFee, his maternal grandmother. "It seemed like grandpa was always fixing the pedals on his bike as a child."

Chris was extremely close to his family. He was fortunate to have grandparents who lived across the street and another set of grandparents who lived in Decatur (about 15 miles away). Chris was the only grandchild in the Taylor family who was old enough to know his Grandfather Taylor. Chris was five years old when his Grandfather Taylor died and many trips were made to Decatur so Grandpa could see Chris anytime, day or night. Grandpa Taylor was in and out of the hospital for over a year before his death and each time he wouldn't consent to being admitted until he had seen his grandson. Even when Chris had grown up he would always make an effort to see his Grandmother Taylor who then lived in Kalamazoo. Her health was failing and he always made an effort to see her when he returned to the Michigan area for a visit.

Because he had grandparents, aunts and uncles living so close, Chris received almost anything within reason a child could want. When he was six years old, he was given a rocking chair for

Christmas; though it was an unusual gift for such a young boy, Chris was fascinated by the rocker and very proud of it.

Chris was also very close to his two sisters. Sherrie was born in 1955 and Becky in 1958. Both girls now own and operate their own floral shops in the Dowagiac area. Becky Taylor Maier owns the Village Floral Shop in Cassopolis and Sherrie owns Taylor's Country Florist located in Paw Paw.

Growing up with a big brother like Chris wasn't always the easiest thing in the world for Sherrie and Becky to accept, as they were known mostly as Chris Taylor's sisters. Yet, they have always been very proud of their older brother and harbor many fond memories of him.

Chris loved to tease and joke with his sisters and to wrestle them...both of them against him. Their best defense was to get him laughing so hard he could hardly breathe. From the mad scramble on the floor to the dining table, they would continue their pursuit to get the best of their giant brother. The girls teamed up to arm wrestle him, the two of them against Chris. The girls always lost. He would form a muscle with his huge arms and ask the girls to do the same with theirs, and then tease them about how they didn't have any muscle.

They remember him as the kind of brother who didn't mind little sisters who wanted to tag along. He would take them with him in the car and hardly ever make them duck down in the car seat, afraid they would embarrass him. He taught his sisters how to roller skate, and the trio went skating almost every weekend.

"Chris could really skate," recalled Sherrie. "We could never skate as well as he did. In the winters we went sledding. With Chris on the back of the sled, we would really go fast."

As a child Chris was pretty much accepted by his peers, but he still drew comments on his size. To his sisters, who were with him so much of the time, he didn't seem abnormal in his size at all. They found it horrible when people gave him a bad time about his size and wouldn't know how to react to the things they heard said to him or about him. Chris learned to ignore much of what was said, and learned to handle situations with patience.

One of his closest friends was Dean Claborn. They were born just six months apart and were together as much as possible for many years. Both had paper routes and they delivered their papers together every night after junior high school. If one was needed for some project, the other would be there to help out. Dean remained close to the entire Taylor family throughout the decades.

As he progressed through childhood and continued to grow, people began to stare at Chris more and more, a plague that strikes most men and women who are even a bit different in appearance from the rest of the world. But Chris learned to ignore much of what was said, and he learned to handle each situation with patience. It was a trait his parents stressed over and over and one that would stand him in good stead as the years rolled by.

"We always taught him not to hit back," said Vera. "Maybe that's why he was so gentle later in his life. When Chris first started to play football he didn't want to hit like the players are supposed to, and I think that was because we told him not to hit anyone when he was a young child."

As a Little League baseball player, Chris played catcher. He also joined the Cub Scouts and Boy Scouts; it was in Boy Scouts where he first learned to swim, taking to the water like a fish. The scout years were a very important stage in Chris's development. He spent many hours in activities that allowed him to interact meaningfully with others his age — if not his size.

A winter campout was set. The tents were pitched. The day's activities came to an end and it was time for the Scouts to settle down for the night.

The Scouts had hung their clothes outside for the night, not knowing that rain was in the forecast. In the morning the clothes had all been soaked with rain and then frozen due to a drop in the temperature. The Scouts had a good laugh about that trip.

As with most large people, more was expected of Chris, especially as a child. Since he matured physically at a more rapid rate than other children his age, he was often placed in the role of being a leader, the one in the group who was expected to take charge. He was often judged to be much older than he actually was.

"The first time I ever saw Chris he must have been about six years old and he was swimming with some other young boys. When he was six or seven he looked like he was starting high school," said Jack McAvoy, his high school football coach. "At the time I thought he was their overseer, not just one of the boys."

As early as the first time Chris was old enough to compete in an organized sport, seventh grade football, his school received phone calls complaining about his size. School officials even received requests he not be allowed to participate in sporting activities, for fear other young athletes could be injured. If the family of young AIDS victim Ryan White suffered from an unreasonable prejudice in 1987 and 1988, making front page national news, so did the

Dowagiac Taylors suffer from similar feelings almost thirty years earlier.

Before his junior high years, Vera felt Chris should be moved from the neighborhood school of McKinley Elementary to Justice Gage Elementary School, a school in another neighborhood. She was convinced he needed to be exposed to a greater number of children who did not know him. At such a formative time in his young life, she hoped that if more children came in contact with Chris, they would get to know him and realize his size was not an indication of his temperament, and was nothing to be afraid of.

In American society, the big guy is all too often portrayed as a villain and perceived as "the bad guy". Once people got to know Chris, most of their reservations evaporated.

As the years passed, Chris continued to grow at an amazing rate. Clothes had to be continually altered, while shoes became difficult to find. And he did present special discipline problems for his parents.

"With Chris the size he was as a child growing up, I learned to use tact, not force on him to convince him to do things," said Jim. "He was just too big to try to use force on."

Life on the family farm, located on Twin Lakes Road in Dowagiac brings back memories of Chris. The 40 acre farm which was a part-time farming venture for the Taylors is a beautiful wooded acreage. Walnut trees, red oak, hickory and wild cherry trees can be found on the rolling hills. Jim raised black angus cattle, pigs and chickens. The girls had their 4-H horses. The split level home sits in the middle of the land.

Living on the farm in Chris's later years required helping out at hay-making time. The group of farm workers were joined by Chris when possible to help out with this seasonal chore. Chris would take two bales of hay and as he threw them on top of the hay rack he would let out a sneeze that could be registered on the Richtor Scale. Chris had a terrible case of hay fever.

As Chris became older, he would tease his sisters more and more about their boyfriends. He would appear, with his big size that he was, which would scare any boy from his sister and ask," And you're going out with my sister?" He always looked out for and loved his sisters very much.

At the age of two his parents couldn't keep him off ladders. A new home was being built and Chris would always be up on the ladder. Since Chris was the first grandchild and having his grandparents live across the street he could do almost anything he wanted to and get away with it, especially when his grandparents were involved.

The Gentle Giant

CHAPTER 3
Growing Up in Dowagiac

Chris's summers during high school found him involved in many activities. He could be found at the Fitch Camp, a children's day camp for the town children. The camp was held at Cable Lake, a small lake about ten miles from Dowagiac. It was a great place for Chris to learn patience and understanding while working with and caring for the children. It was something that Chris looked forward to each summer, spending time with the children, which carried over into his adult life.

Chris also worked at a small dance hall just outside of Dowagiac as a bouncer during the summer months when he was in high school. The dance hall was located just five miles from town at a well known land mark referred to as the Five Mile Corner. It was a jumping place frequented with Chicago folks who came into the Lakes area for a good time.

Chris would take his sisters and their girlfriends along with him every once in awhile. The girls looked forward to the summer dances and it was for sure that no one would mess around with Chris Taylor's sisters. Even if someone would be creating a problem, Chris never found the need to become rough with anyone; he would simply talk to the trouble makers and get them to shake hands and forget about what had happened or ask them to leave. His size was intimidating and he would tell his sisters that it would be okay if they were to have boyfriends, but they would have to "whip" him first. Not too much of a request...no problem.

Chris entered high school at Dowagiac Union High School as a freshman in 1965. The late Homas Smull was the high school principal and Carl Shopbell was the superintendent of schools. Jack McAvoy, now athletic director at Hillsdale College in Hillsdale, Michigan, was Chris's world history teacher and football coach.

"It was my pleasure to coach Chris Taylor his sophomore and junior years on the Dowagiac High School football teams. Naturally, as a freshman he played on the freshman team. When Chris was six or seven years old he looked like he was starting high school. He was easy going, bright and a pleasure to be around."

As a freshman football player, the freshman coaches used Chris as a fullback in one of the games. Chris weighed 250-300 pounds at the time. McAvoy had to ask the coaches to put him back in the line on offense where he belonged so he wouldn't hurt anyone. Chris was real happy about that as well.

After a couple of games on the junior varsity level Chris's sophomore year, he was moved up to varsity and played noseguard in an Oklahoma 5-2 defense as well as centering the ball on offense. Needless to say, the middle of the defensive line was fully protected by Chris's presence. He was quick for a big man but only for a few steps, then he would run out of gas.

Chris earned a junior varsity letter in football and was recognized in the "Wahoo", the Dowagiac High School Yearbook, for participating in chorus, as well. But he didn't compete in wrestling his freshman year.

With the persuasion of wrestling coach John Lewis, Chris went out for the wrestling team as a sophomore. He quickly discovered he was "King Cowboy," so much so that he neglected his chores at home and was treating everyone with great impatience around the house. His wrestling season was about to come to an end.

The team was in the wrestling room working out one night when Jim Taylor walked in. He had warned Chris that either things would be done around the farm as expected, or Chris's wrestling career would be short-lived.

Jim walked over to Chris and said," Son, you're going home; get your things."

Chris never said a word. He gathered his belongings and left with his dad. As much as his parents regretted such severe action, they had a lesson they wanted their son to learn. Chris was pulled from the wrestling squad that year, and things settled back to normal at home.

In an incident Chris's junior year in high school, Chris walked into the office of his wrestling coach. He was upset because some of the other athletes chided him about the weigh-in procedure. The school's scale only went to the 300 pound limit and it was upsetting to Chris when a couple of the guys wanted to rent a larger scale.

Another time while Chris was a junior, it was required that all the athletes at the beginning of the football season had to run the half mile in a certain time. The time was assessed according to the athlete's position. Chris navigated the track twice successfully, and in the time it took to qualify. That junior season, 1967, Dowagiac boasted the largest tackles in the nation on the high school level. Chris was at one side, checking in at 375 pounds and his friend, Craig Behnke, was on the other side, at 300 pounds. It was extremely difficult for opposing backs to run off tackle, or over tackle. The

Photo by Charlie Blue

The 1967 Dowagiac varsity football team, conference co-champs with a record of 7-2-0.

team posted a record of 7-1-1 and scored 201 points to their opponents' 61.

During the Coldwater-Dowagiac football game, Chris came off the field at the halftime of the game, limping and grimacing.

"My knee hurts," said Chris.

"What's the matter with your knee?" asked McAvoy.

"The kid playing across from me keeps hitting me in the knee with his helmet," said Chris.

"Oh, you mean that player they took away in the ambulance to the hospital just after the half?" asked McAvoy. "He has a concussion from hitting your knee."

Opposing teams learned to double team Chris, or pull to his opposite side during the games. It was the only way to play against the Dowagiac giant — because it was impossible to go around him, over him or through him. Chris also played in the backfield sometimes, a fullback in the mold of "The Fridge" of Chicago Bears' 1985 fame. Like the 330 pound William Perry, Taylor plowed straight ahead, sometimes up to five opposing players hanging onto his huge thighs.

When Chris assumed the regular "set" position to block, he would be half standing up. He was so big that even in a normal stance he stood a full head taller than anyone else on the team. He was considered the key player in the Dowagiac Union High School defense that season. Opposing blockers found the big guy a block of granite that would not budge. Yet, he wasn't accorded any post-season honors.

Football was not the only athletic talent Chris had. As a sophomore he competed on the track team as a shot putter, hitting the 48 foot, five inch mark. The effort was good enough for fifth place in the Western Regional track competition.

When Chris went out for wrestling as a junior, the biggest problem facing the coach was to find athletes large enough to give him adequate competition to work out with in the wrestling room, a problem that would plague him all his career. Often, two athletes wrestled him at the same time during practices, plus once in awhile former athletes from the community came to work out with him.

Chris's strength continued to amaze everyone. Even his own father was surprised at the strength his son exhibited one day while taking pigs to market. One of the pigs fell off the back of the pickup truck. His father stopped the truck, and the two of them walked around to the back.

"Now, just how are we going to get that animal back onto the truck?" asked Jim.

"That's no problem," said Chris, grabbing the pig and hoisting it back into the truck by himself.

Impressed, Jim marked the pig. He wanted to see how much it weighed. When they arrived at market, the pig tipped the scales at 255 pounds. It was one of the first indications of the prodigious strength that lurked in Chris's massive body, and the first time Jim began to fully comprehend how special his son really was.

Chris had a great junior year on the wrestling mat and his reputation began to grow by leaps and bounds. He was already looked upon as "The Gentle Giant" at several nearby schools, including Niles High School. The wrestling coach at Niles, Ed Weede, considered Chris a great high school athlete who could have easily hurt people if he had tried, but Weede felt Chris was always aware of the potential for injury and wrestled accordingly. He would win and make it as painless as possible.

When Dowagiac wrestled Niles, Weede told his heavyweight the score going into the final match would determine if Niles would forfeit at heavyweight. But when the 165 pound match started Weede couldn't locate his heavyweight anywhere. He slipped into the locker room, and found his wrestler out of uniform.

"What are you doing?" asked Weede.

"I'm changing into my clothes, there is no way I'm going to wrestle Taylor, no-how," the wrestler replied.

The Dowagiac Chief wrestlers compiled a 10-45-1 record Chris's junior year, winning six straight dual meets before losing to Niles,

33-13. The team placed fourth in the Big 6 Conference meet held at Portage Northern.

The Chiefs took third in the regional and Chris was a third place finisher, as well, losing in the semifinals. Not gaining the regional finals undoubtedly served as a motivating factor to make him even more determined to win it all at the state tournament in Lansing. Chris and his teammates, Charlie Garrett, wrestling at 180 pounds, and Craig Cline, 133 pounds, had all qualified for the state meet. Garrett entered the meet as a three-time Big 6 Champion and was the number one seed.

Chris wrestling in high school with friend Wiley.

Chris was by far the biggest man in the tournament in the heavyweight division, at an estimated 365 pounds. It was impossible to get an accurate reading because the scale only registered up to 360 pounds.

In his opening match, Chris was pitted against the number one seed, Ben Lewis of Fenton, who was undefeated. Chris won in a hard-fought 6-5 battle.

The rest of the tournament was relatively easy for "The Giant" from Dowagiac. But he was still one match away from the top of hill. Soon, he hoped, he would be king of that hill, not on the playground, or even in the wrestling room, but this time on the top of the state of Michigan.

The final match of the day had come for Chris. He was faced with Tom Eiden of Lansing Gabriels. The top was looking even closer as the two entered the third and final period of wrestling. With just 13 seconds ticked off the clock in that final period of wrestling, Chris was the winner by a pin. He had done it, as a junior and his true first year of wrestling, Chris had finished the season off with a state championship. He had compiled a remarkable 25-1 season, with only that one blemish when he had finished third place at the regional competition.

The two Chief wrestlers had compiled 32 points for a fourth place finish as a team. What a team, the two finishing the highest ever for a Dowagiac wrestling team. It looked as though Chris Taylor was on the way to making a name for himself in the world of wrestling. Little did anyone know that he would eventually become a hero of sorts to wrestlers all over the world and eventually win the bronze medal in the Olympic Games. The dream of every athlete to compete on an Olympic level of competition would someday come true for Chris Taylor.

Chris's senior year at Dowagiac High School found him busy with studies and sports. This was the year to start thinking about college. Every major college in the United States who had a successful wrestling team would soon be knocking on his door. But this was the year to have a good time and participate in the sports he so dearly loved...football and wrestling.

The 7-2-0 Chief football team was sparked by Chris, Craig Cline, Charlie Blue and Doug Greenwood on the defensive line. It was a good year for Chris as he was a game captain leading his fellow teammates throughout the season.

Wrestling season came around and the team ran up some pretty impressive stats. They compiled a record 14-3-1. They made school history with a first place finish in the regional Class B wrestling tournament which was held at Sturgis, Michigan.

Chris helped lead the way for the Chiefs, weighing in at a high of 391 pounds. He was undefeated, a defending state champion and he was on his way one more time.

Chris pinned Buchanan's Roger Hassen with just 38 seconds left on the clock to wrap up the Sturgis Class B crown. Chris and four other Chiefs would go after the state crown the following Friday and Saturday at Wyoming Gowin Heights in Wyoming, Michigan. Joining Chris on the trip to the state meet were Dan VanHusan who had won first place at 95 pounds, Walt Hill who had also won a first at 103 pounds, Charlie Blue with yet another first place at 180 pounds and Ken Bell with a second place finish at 127 pounds.

The first place finish at the regional had been a close battle. The Brandywine Bobcats and the Chiefs were deadlocked with only two matches remaining in the meet, but the victories from Blue and Taylor clinched the crown for the Chiefs. The boys laughed on the way home from the meet. Chris and his friends sat in the back of the bus on the ride home that night. It was told that Coach Lewis would not allow anyone who lost at a meet to laugh on the way home from a meet. That night they laughed...but then Chris always laughed.

The Gentle Giant

The state meet was only a few days away. The five wrestlers would work hard to get ready for the big meet. This would be Chris's second appearance at the state level and again he was excited about the thought of possibly being a two-time Michigan prep champion.

Again the Chiefs would find themselves in the history book at Dowagiac High School. The team took a second place finish overall. And for Chris, he too had to settle for second best.

It was an overtime match that took the gold medal from Chris. This time Ben Lewis came out on top with the first place finish. A rematch from the previous year, Lewis won the overtime match with a 1-0 score. He had lost only one time in his prep career, that was to Chris in the finals of the state meet the year before. This time the shoe was on the other foot.

Chris pinned Roger Hunt from Harpers Creek in just 56 seconds. He had won by a 4-0 decision over David Conklin of Northville and he had won an 8-2 decision over Cedar Springs Barry Melanowski. His senior year had come to an end with a 33-1 record. Chris's buddy Charlie Blue had also won a second place medal.

Chris and Charlie had waited in the locker room together before they each took to the mat for their final bout that day. They sat, listening and watching, and taking in what the other wrestlers were saying.

A wrestler in the locker room stood up and asked the two, "What are you two doing in here?" he asked.

"Why we are waiting for our turn to wrestle," responded Chris.

The wrestlers laughed and announced that they were getting ready to wrestle in the consolation round.

Big Chris stood up, moved toward the wrestlers and in his deep voice commanded, "Well, we are getting ready to wrestle in the finals." End of conversation.

Chris and Charlie watched each other get beat in those finals. They were feeling pretty lousy and returned to the locker room to get ready for the trip home. Chris looked at Charlie and said, "At least we got a trophy and a medal...we won't have to go out and buy our own." They both laughed, remembering something that had happened the week previous at the regional competition.

It was at regionals that Chris and Charlie decided to take a break from all the pressures of wrestling. They took a walk to the business area in the town to find some banana cream pie (the two were known for their banana cream pie cravings) and there seemed to be enough time before the finals for a slice.

While out on their walk they detoured to a trophy shop to

check out the medals. After all, back in those days medals were hard to come by in wrestling. The two thought it not a bad idea to purchase a few.

However it was just a thought when the two were out that day, as they returned without any additional hardware on their chests. They did return to the regional competition to win their own first place medals.

Back at the state meet, the boys were getting ready for the trip home. It was a silent ride, but that silence was soon broken. Coach Lewis took his team to the first restaurant he would find. The team entered, taking their state trophy with them. They set it in the center of the table and ordered their food. As people in the restaurant noticed the team they offered to buy their food for them and after the bill was paid the team still had $35 left in their food fund.

The state tournament brought a vivid memory for yet another coach from Sturgis High School, Bart Kruse. Kruse was the wrestling coach for Sturgis and was attending the state meet.

The Sturgis High School wrestling coach remembers Chris Taylor through a sad memory. It was the memory of Chris after his championship match with Ben Lewis.

Chris was sitting in the corner after his match. He was sitting there all by himself. There were tears streaming down his cheeks. He was naturally upset with his loss, but was more disturbed because it seemed like the whole crowd was against him. He couldn't understand that.

"Chris, these people aren't opposed to you, they don't even know you," said Kruse to Chris. "They seemed opposed to your size, I suppose like that of a professional wrestling villain," added Kruse.

Chris just sat and listened.

If those people at that meet would have gotten to know him, they would have been his fans then like they became later.

Chris was remembered to this coach as the "Gentle Giant" and commented that he never knew Chris to do anything close to being dirty, unsportsmanlike or anything to embarrass anyone.

Chris was one of eleven graduating seniors on the wrestling team. They would need to be replaced in the next season. It would take a big man in many ways to replace the presence of Chris Taylor on the Chief wrestling team.

Charlie Blue received the varsity wrestling award and Chuck Burling shared the highest award, the All Sports Award, with Chris. The two, Chris and Charlie, had been close for a long time. The friendship began in junior high school. The two were in the same class, but Charlie lived in the country and Chris was living in town at that time. They mainly saw each other in school and became good friends. Both participated in the same sports throughout their high school careers.

Chris and Chuck went back somewhat farther in time. The two had attended Fitch Camp and played Little League baseball together. In fact Chris was catching for the A's team when Chuck hit his first home run off Delmar Gillman. The two went to Cub Scout outings together and when the junior high years hit they became very close friends and they played on the same football team.

Chris and Chuck finished a senior year of having a successful season at every sport they participated in. It was impossible for those making the selection for the 1968 All Sports winner to narrow the selection to only one athlete, so for the first time since the inception of the award in 1950, two would be named.

Chuck Burling with the 1968 All Sports Award.

The 1968 winners were Chris Taylor and Chuck Burling. They shared the coveted honor as they listened to Notre Dame head basketball coach John Dee share words of wisdom with the banquet guests. "You are the cream of the crop in this community because you are athletes," he began. "Once you've taken on the identity as an athlete, people expect a little more from you."

More rain fell in Chris Taylor's young life. The death of a long-time friend weighed heavy on Chris. John "Randy" Huscher was killed in Vietnam. His life was ended when he stepped on a land mine. The 19 year old had been killed in action. His mother, Mrs. Bill Bennett had been notified that he had been reported missing in action. Eventually that report had been changed to say that Randy had been killed in action. He was the first Dowagiac man to die in the Vietnam War.

Randy and Chris had grown up together and had delivered the *Dowagiac Daily News* together. Both were well known to the people in Dowagiac.

"The death of Randy was really tough on Chris," commented Chuck Burling, now an established dentist in Dowagiac. "He lost a dear friend and it bothered him."

Chris would often visit Randy's grave in Niles, Michigan. He made frequent visits to the grave site and was finding it difficult to cope with Randy's death. In fact, Chris visited Randy's grave shortly before his own death. He never got over the death of his childhood friend.

Photo courtesy of the Dowagiac Daily News

Chris and Harry Shepard at Elks Pancake Breakfast in Dowagiac, MI.

The All Sports Banquet was the perfect ending to an almost perfect senior year for Chris. He had lost in the state wrestling finals and he had lost one of his best friends to a war that was not easily understood or accepted by so many Americans. But sharing the All Sports Award with yet another good friend seemed fitting to Chris. The trophy for the evening went home with Chuck. Chris wanted it that way. That was the way Chris was. It meant more to him to have his best friend have the trophy than it did for him to keep it himself. The wrestler... "The Gentle Giant"...the kind man...the best friend...that was the Chris Taylor known to his friends.

Not only did his friends think of Chris as a caring person, but Jim Hunter, who is in his 23rd year of teaching science and math at Dowagiac High School thought of Chris this way:

"I had Chris in school in his junior and senior years. He was a very kind and gentle person in spite of his size. He never showed anger and never seemed to get upset," said the school teacher.

Chris was an even-tempered person who seemed like he didn't have a problem in the world. Chris was a person with a multitude of friends who liked Chris for himself.

"I remember sometimes Chris would have to turn sideways in the doorway to get through. His size was something that he dealt with on a daily basis. One time in the science lab Chris was sitting on top of one of the tables and it broke. But he just laughed it off. You know, I think that you would look forever and fail to find anyone who would have an unkind word to say about Chris Taylor," he concluded.

CHAPTER 4
Lynne Hart Enters the Picture

Lynne Hart was walking down a hall in one of the buildings at Muskegon Community College one day during the fall semester of her freshman year when she noticed a student approaching from the opposite direction. He was wearing a letter jacket with the letter "D" on it. What made him so different from the other students in the hall was his size. He was huge; and where, she wondered, would he have come from with that "D" on his jacket.

"It must be from Detroit," she said to herself. She shook her head and turned to watch Chris Taylor amble past. It was obvious Chris had not noticed her, but she couldn't help but notice him. His size was reason enough to take a second look, but there was something else about him that caught her attention.

Born in Muskegon to Robert and Frances Hart, Lynne graduated from Muskegon High School in 1968 and enrolled the following fall at Muskegon Community College. As there was no housing of students at the two-year junior college, she remained living at the family home, on 13 acres in the country.

Chris graduated in 1968, and wasn't totally convinced he was college material. But others felt quite differently. Several of the top wrestling coaches in the nation were knocking at his door, trying to entice him to enter their universities. He discussed his feelings and his options with his parents, and at last decided to stay close to home. He had been an average student in a small town — and somehow the thought of attending a big university was too much for Chris at this time in his life.

He entered Muskegon Community College in the fall of 1968 with the hope he could transfer at the end of two years to study forestry and conservation at a major university. He also entered junior college determined to continue his wrestling career.

He made the Jayhawk wrestling team with ease. His coach at Muskegon Community College was Sid Huitema and the group of wrestlers who entered with Chris would eventually set new standards for the school.

As a freshman Chris was considered a "Goliath" at many of the tournaments he wrestled at. He was now six foot, five inches tall and weighed close to 400 pounds. He rolled up a 12-0 dual meet record, with 11 pins during his first season as a Jayhawk wrestler. His most impressive showing came at the prestigious Midlands Tournament in LaGrange, Illinois. The tournament is considered America's toughest because it allows postgraduates to compete with the collegiate athletes. The field of 426 was loaded with former national champions and ex-Olympians.

Throughout the tournament hall the question, "Hey, did the giant win?" echoed time after time. Taylor battled to the semifinals before losing 3-2 to Greg Wojciechowski, of Toledo, one of the nations highest regarded matmen at the NCAA level. Chris also lost his third place match to Dale Stearns, from the University of Iowa.

He shook off the disappointment of the two losses at the Midlands, and closed out the dual meet season with a perfect 18-0 mark. At the 10th annual National Junior College Wrestling Championships

Chris with his dad, Jim, during the 10th Annual National Junior College Wrestling Championships.

The Gentle Giant

Chris, along with Bill Fjelind, Carl Adams, Les Anderson and Ben Peterson at an awards ceremony.

in Worthington, Minnesota, he led the team to a seventh place finish. Chris gained the finals with four straight wins and won the championship with a 3-2 triumph over defending champion Harry Geris of Joliet, Illinois. The match marked the beginning of a long rivalry between Chris and Geris, who moved on to Oklahoma State.

Teammate Mike Shearer, a fellow Dowagiac Union High School wrestler, also took top honors in Worthington for the Jayhawks. Shearer was 30-0 going into the tournament at 123 pounds and posted a 7-0 decision in the finals. The Jayhawks scored 40 points, a tremendous accomplishment for a school in its second year of wrestling.

Chris and Shearer became the first wrestlers from the state of Michigan to win national titles in the Junior College Athletic Association. And Chris had piled up an impressive record on his way. Besides placing fourth at the Midlands, he had won titles at Hiram Tournament, Detroit Freestyle Open and the Michigan Junior College Championships.

He also set the record at Muskegon Community College for the most pins in a season with eleven (and, subsequently, the most pins for two years with 21, the most wins in dual meets with 21 and the most career wins with 36).

The second semester at Muskegon Community College found Lynne Hart spending more and more time in the gym. And with good reason. She was a member of the women's basketball and volleyball teams and was studying physical education. She again noticed the big guy from the hallway, and they conversed briefly on several occasions. They even shot a few baskets together.

"My first impression of Chris was that of an arrogant wrestler," said Lynne years later.

That opinion didn't last long, however. Once when the women's basketball team wanted to scrimmage, the wrestlers came off the mat, eager to assist. Taking her girls aside, the coach told them, "Don't worry about the big guy."

Lynne was a seasoned guard and knew the position well. She was confident she could contain about anybody; that is, until she began guarding Chris.

Lynne watched the rest of the team race up the court. Then when she spun around to take off, she slammed into Chris—and bounced off. It was the start of something big. The two often laughed later about never really having a first date. But they enjoyed one another's company and began spending weekends on the Taylor family farm in Dowagiac.

Chris rolled off 21 straight victories his sophomore year at Muskegon Community College. He had a perfect record of 21-0 and finished first at the Michigan AAU and the Michigan Junior College Championships.

There was tragedy again in Chris's life. Chris, was responsible for injuries to two other wrestlers, both happening in the same week. One was so devastating that he almost gave up the sport for good.

It was late in the afternoon, and practice had just begun. The wrestlers were finishing their warm-ups and Chris and Charlie Blue were sparring with each other, getting ready for serious practice to begin. As Chris shot in for a takedown, Blue tried to counter the move and his foot caught in the wrestling mat. His body twisted and Blue screamed out in pain. He passed out on the wrestling mat. His twisted leg was beneath him. He awoke in the locker room with ice on his knee and Chris at his side.

Chris had carried Blue up two flights of stairs and helped him into the shower. He also helped him gather his belongings and then drove him to the hospital. Surgery was scheduled for the following morning, and Chris continued to stay by his friend's side. He visited him twice a day while he was hospitalized and after Blue was dismissed, Chris acted as his chauffeur, giving him rides around town.

Blue's knee recovered, but another wrestler fell to an injury the same week. This time, it was far more serious, and the wrestler did not have a full recovery. Jim Stibitz and Chris were in the midst of practice session; Stibitz shot in for a takedown, and Chris countered. They hit the mat, and the room went silent as the wrestlers realized something horrible had happened. The accident left Stibitz paralyzed for life.

The two injuries nearly ended Chris's career. He was ready to toss in the towel and never wrestle again. He was devastated by the thought he had caused two accidents with his size and contemplated dropping out of school right on the spot. It was a week that would live with him the rest of his life.

He left campus and went home to Dowagiac to do some soul searching. He told his best friend, Chuck Burling, about the accident and they discussed it at great length. Finally, he told Burling he was not going to wrestle any more.

But with the encouragement of friends and his family and from Stibitz's father, Chris returned to school and continued to wrestle. It was Stibitz's father who finally convinced Chris it was an accident and that he should not give up wrestling.

Chris entered the National Junior College Championships at Worthington, Minnesota, as the defending champion at heavyweight. Huitema had talked the local Dodge dealer into letting the team use a motor home for the trip. On the drive to Worthington, the team stopped at Iowa State University in Ames. Dr. Harold Nichols, the Iowa State coach, had invited the team to work out in the ISU wrestling room. It was there that Nichols saw Chris for the first time.

Chris worked out in the Iowa State wrestling room and Nichols asked Huitema to call him after the nationals were over to let him know how Chris had fared. Nichols was interested in Chris...and would eventually become the determining factor as to where Chris would further his college education.

Muskegon was in first place with 61 points at the end of the first day's competition. Three of five Jayhawks had advanced to the finals — but Chris was not one of them. The biggest upset in the tournament came in the semifinals, when Chris lost an 8-3 decision to Tom Murry of Lake County.

Chris finished third and was awarded the Gorriaran Trophy for the most pins – four – in the least aggregate time. In his consolation battle for third place, he flattened Paul Wagner of Fulton in 4:59. In addition, his teammates Doug Lee (118), Larry Arnold (142) and Roger Duty (150) all lost in the finals.

Despite the huge upset at heavyweight, and the fact that Muskegon did not crowned a single champion, the Jayhawks captured the team title. The trophy Huitema and his ten wrestlers

NCAA Wrestling Champions University of Washington

brought back to Muskegon was only the second national athletic championship in ten years, as the cross country team took a first place in 1960. The wrestling championship was recognized by association officials as the first national title in that sport for any Michigan team since the association was organized.

The collegiate season was over, but Chris entered the National AAU Freestyle Tournament in April in Lincoln, Nebraska. His only loss came by a 5-3 score to the eventual champion, Toledo's Greg Wojciechowski, the same man who had defeated him at the Midlands Tournament the previous December. It was Taylor's first match of the meet and he didn't lose again, finishing second.

He scored a decision over Jeff Smith, a two-time All American at Michigan State, and wiped out a California junior college champion with a pin in 20 seconds. He also won by forfeit over a wrestler who failed to show up for the match.

A week later, he discovered Greco-Roman wrestling, the sport that only allows holds above the waist. He won the heavyweight title at the national AAU meet in Columbia Heights, Minnesota, a suburb of Minneapolis.

"I found that Greco-Roman was great for me because you can only use your upper body in takedowns, whereas in freestyle wrestling you can use your legs," said Chris. "Most of my strength and good moves come from the top portion of my body. I think that's why I've enjoyed success in this form of wrestling."

His performance at the Greco-Roman nationals earned him a spot on the United States team that competed in the world championships in Edmonton, Canada. At age 20, it was his first taste of international competition. He opened up with a 25-second pin, but then lost twice on decisions. Despite just one win, he finished fourth in the small field.

"He was not a favorite with the fans, although his bouts drew the most interest," reported one writer at the scene. "Taylor, however, has learned to live with his unusual dimensions. He looks mean, but has an alarmingly soft voice and is one of the most likeable wrestlers at the meet. He would hold people's children in one hand for photographs.

"Chris had gone through his first international competition smiling, until the final defeat when he sat on a chair next to the ring for three minutes with his head buried in a towel, completely immersed in perspiration.

" 'I'm discouraged,' he said. 'I've never wrestled anyone like Martinesco from Romania before.'"

"After several minutes of silence he flashed a smile and said, 'I'll feel better tomorrow.'

"Chris was good, but he was lacking experience. He was unquestionably the biggest man to wrestle for the United States in the history of the sport. He moves well and is extremely agile."

The powerful Romanian, Nicolae Martinesco, finished third in the world tournament, behind a Soviet and a Hungarian, but had handled Chris with ease. It was a sobering introduction to world-class wrestling for the youngster just two years out of Dowagiac Union High School.

In the meantime, Chris had acquired a new fan; the girl from the basketball team had now become a good friend. In fact they were now more than just friends, they were dating.

Chris had lots of friends, but never a serious girlfriend...that is until he met Lynne Hart. He hadn't been big on dating in high school or since he came to junior college either. He seemed to enjoy groups of people more than one-on-one situations.

There had been two girls in Chris's life during high school, one was Terry Huff who Chris dated on and off for two years and the other was Sue Behnke who was a very close friend.

Sue and Chris were very good friends. He would help her with her government and would always come to visit her when he came home from junior college. The two spent time playing cards at Tom and Joyce Nugent's house. Good times, lots of laughs and spending time with friends filled the days and evenings on those visits home.

But for the present time, Lynne Hart was on the scene and would be around for a good many wrestling meets down the road.

The long season was finally over, and so was the school year. Lynne was working the summer at a 4-H camp as a cook and counselor. Camp officials needed someone to help start campfires and to work as a handyman, and they asked Lynne if she knew of someone who needed a summer job, and Chris applied for it.

The first day on the job was a hot one for Chris; he spent the entire day carrying watermelons into the camp cooler. Lynne felt sorry for him: "The poor guy is sweating bullets," she thought.

"I think I'll just sleep in here at the end of the day," Chris told her, pointing at the cooler and wiping the huge drops of sweat from his forehead.

They spent considerable time talking with one another around the campfire at the end of each day, and got to know each other much better. But when the job was over, Chris went his own way, and they didn't see each other the rest of the summer.

The summer of 1970 found Chris facing one of the most important decisions of his life. Several major colleges had offered him wrestling scholarships, and he was struggling with the decision.

"I have the size and strength it takes and I enjoy the spirit of competition," he told a friend.

"I have certain goals I want to accomplish as an amateur and then I hope to use wrestling as a way of setting up a nest egg before I go into my chosen profession."

And another long-range goal had forced its way into his consciousness: "I'm shooting for an Olympic championship," he said.

With that thought in mind, there were only a handful of colleges in the United States where he could obtain the coaching and the workouts that would allow him to progress enough in his wrestling to be a factor in the 1972 Olympic trials, scarcely two years away. Chris began taking a real hard look at the options available to him.

Chris on a recruiting trip to Arizona.

The Gentle Giant

CHAPTER 5
Wearing the Cardinal and Gold

Iowa State University has long been regarded as one of the most beautiful colleges in the United States. The sprawling campus in Ames, a city of approximately 45,000 population, includes more than 100 major buildings. It boasts a park like setting, with its best known symbol, the Campanile, serving as a focal point since 1899.

Located in the center of the state, Ames is just thirty miles north of Des Moines, the state capital. Ames was platted and named in 1864, and prospered in great part because of the stature achieved by ISU. Though Ames offers all of the educational and cultural opportunities associated with a major university, it has managed to preserve a style of living seldom found in more densely populated centers.

The college has not been a bastion of athletic greatness, except in wrestling. The legendary Charles Mayser formed a wrestling team in 1916, and for the next seven decades only three men coached the Cyclones in wrestling. Mayser, Hugo Otopalik and Dr. Harold Nichols are all members of the National Wrestling Hall of Fame, in Stillwater, Oklahoma — but it was Nichols who led Iowa State to its greatest heights.

Born and raised in Cresco, a small farm community in northern Iowa, Nichols captured an NCAA title for the University of Michigan as a 145 pounder in 1939. He coached at Arkansas State for six years before taking over at Iowa State in 1954. The Nichols era lasted 35 years, and produced 456 dual meet victories and scores of All-Americans. In 1965, he led ISU to its first ever NCAA team title. And his Cyclones repeated as NCAA champions in 1969 and 1970. By the time Chris was searching for a college, Iowa State was one of the two premier wrestling powers in the nation.

But Chris seemed to be leaning toward Arizona State and Oklahoma State. While Arizona State offered the great Southwest, Oklahoma State, proud possessor of 26 NCAA team titles, competed with Iowa State for the reputation as the nation's top wrestling school. What Chris needed most of all, however, was a workout room that could offer suitable training partners. According to an old maxim, wrestlers are only as good as their workout partners, and it holds particularly true in the case of heavyweights.

The determining factor in Chris's decision may have been the 1969 Midlands Tournament. There, competing against the nation's best, he finished fourth. He was defeated by the powerful Greg Wojciechowski of Toledo in the semifinals, and then lost the third-place battle to Iowa's Dale Stearns. In the finals that night, he watched from the stands as Wojciechowski fell to former Iowa State star Tom Peckham. The rugged Peckham, who never took a backward step during his entire career, had won NCAA titles for Nichols at 177, and weighed just 205 when he took the Midlands heavyweight title. He was employed by Nichols in the wrestling equipment business, and was a regular in the ISU practice room. If a wrestler's goal was to get tough, he could hardly ask for a better workout partner than Tom Peckham.

Then there was Ed Huffman. A former heavyweight state champion for Ames High School, Huffman was a freshman at ISU when he first met Chris at the 1969 Midlands. They were opponents who were destined to become best friends.

"When he walked out on the mat to wrestle me, he was the biggest guy I'd ever seen," recalled Huffman nearly twenty years later. "I was 220, he was about 400. I thought he was just another big guy. I didn't know he was so agile, that he had such superior strength. More strength than anyone I ever saw. He beat me in a close match.

"I think Chris was leaning toward Oklahoma State. Then in springtime, Peckham knocked on the door to my trailer. He had Chris with him, and told me to let him move in with me, that Chris was coming to Iowa State. I took the big bedroom, and gave him the small one," Huffman added with a chuckle.

"I wrestled him every night for two years. We became inseparable. I got up over 300 pounds, too. I'll tell you this — Chris was great, but I never saw him beat Peckham in the room. Not once. That Peckham was one tough guy, the toughest man I've ever known."

There was one other factor in the big decision Chris was facing. He was several credit hours short of qualifying for a four-year school. Nichols assessed his transcript, and found an incomplete grade. He contacted the class instructor at Muskegon, told him of Chris's dilemma, and asked if Chris could make up the incomplete. The instructor agreed, Chris did so, and was eligible to transfer.

The combination of terrific workout partners and Nichols's efforts to help him get in a major college won the day. Chris decided to wrestle for Iowa State. But when he told Lynne of his choice, he couldn't resist adding a twist of Chris Taylor humor to the story.

"I was wondering why you chose ISU when schools like Oklahoma, Oklahoma State, Arizona State, Franklin and Marshall plus so

Chris on the bench at ISU.

Photo courtesy of Sports Illustrated.

The Chris Taylor Story

many more are out there for you to chose from?" asked Lynne.

"I like the looks of their letter jackets," Chris replied, "and I got a look at those uniforms and those robes they wear. They are nice colors, I really like those colors."

He paused, and then added a more serious line: "But what really helped me to decided was Iowa State wrestling coach, Harold Nichols. Dr. Nichols is a coach who really cares about his wrestlers."

Chris was on scholarship, and ISU athletes were left to make the decision as to where they wanted to live. He opted for a motel-apartment complex, The Colonial Inn, located on Lincoln Highway on the east side of Ames, away from campus. It wasn't that Chris was a loner; in fact, it was quite the opposite. The Colonial Inn was a haven for a wide assortment of characters, wrestlers and non-wrestlers alike, providing an atmosphere where Chris felt comfort-able. And once Chris made his presence known at ISU he was sel-dom alone.

After declaring for Iowa State, Chris's size presented a rather unique problem for ISU. A new uniform, bigger than anything ever before constructed for an Cyclone athlete, had to be fashioned.

"We made Chris's uniform right here at Nichols Wrestling Prod-ucts," said Nichols, who had owned and operated one of the nation's most successful wrestling uniform and equipment companies for years. "I took the extra large pattern we had for both singlet and the robe, and just cut it much wider and it fit him fine. The robe was easy for Chris to get in and out of with his size. I think that's why he liked our uniforms so well."

The uniform and Chris's huge workout clothes also became the object of a number of jokes and pranks in the ISU practice room.

"We had fun with Chris," said former teammate Bill Fjetland, head wrestling coach at Algona (Iowa) High School, in 1988. "One time Steve Lampe, who was about 118 pounds, and Larry Munger, who was about 126 pounds, each got in a leg of Chris's warm-ups and came out onto the mat to wrestle.

We heard he was tough but he was so very gentle," added Fjetland. "I can never, ever remember seeing Chris out of control. He was laid back and even tempered; it took quite a bit to get him upset."

The same semester Chris enrolled at Iowa State, Lynne started at Western Michigan University. Michigan proved to be too far from Ames, however, and the separation was short-lived. Lynne moved to Ames in November of 1971 to be near the gentle giant she had be-come so fond of, and found a job working at Younkers Department

The arrival of Chris Taylor was big news in Iowa. Pictured left to right are assistant coach Les Anderson, head coach Harold Nichols and Chris.

Store in the North Grand Shopping Mall.

The arrival of Chris Taylor was big news in Iowa, which appreciates wrestling like few other states. Before he even wrestled a match for ISU, he was featured in a major story in the *Des Moines Register*, the state's largest newspaper. The subject, of course, was his weight...and the fact that he was weighed on the livestock scale at the campus meat lab because no other scale on campus would do the job.

"This is a little too heavy for me," he told a reporter, after being weighed at 416. "I don't like to get up this high, but I haven't wrestled for two months and the only way I can lose weight is by working out. I've tried dieting and that doesn't work for me."

The season started off with a win for Chris at the Southern Open Invitational at the University of Chattanooga, November 26. Chris's path to the finals was paved with three falls and a decision. He pinned Bruce Hart from Moorhead State in 1:12, Bob Johnson from Florida in 3:22 and Harry Geris from Oklahoma State in 1:30 in the final match. He also scored a 3-1 decision over Bill Struve of Oklahoma.

The meet marked the first championship as an Iowa State Cyclone for Chris. He was also awarded the trophy for the most falls in the least amount of time, totaling 6:02. Teammates Carl Adams

Chris's westling debut in Ames.

Photo courtesy of Ames Tribune

(167) and Ben Peterson (190) also won titles for the Cyclones.

His wrestling debut in Ames came in a dual meet with Nebraska. Chris took to the mat like a fish to water and scored a 49 second pin over Chuck Tremain. He flipped his opponent over, held his shoulders to the mat and looked up for the "go ahead" sign from a Cyclone cheerleader. The cheerleader nodded her head and Chris, sporting a wide grin, applied the pressure to score the pin. He was just one of four Cyclones with pins that night, as Phil Parker, Rich Binek and Peterson each contributed six points to the 43-0 romp.

Next, Chris tore through the Iowa State Invitational on December 10 and 11, pinning Don Bonner of Drake University in 27 seconds, Kevin Immel of Winona State in 49 seconds, Mike Thomas of Iowa State in 2:23 and another Cyclone teammate, Steve Clark in 1:43.

During the Christmas season, Chris and Ed Huffman visited the mall to see Lynne at work. With the holiday season, Lynne was extremely busy and the two decided to play a trick on the store Santa greeting the children. Huffman was the first to approach the whiskered, red-suited old gentleman.

"I have this little boy with me who wants to come see you and sit on your lap," said Huffman innocently.

"Well, you just go get him," came the reply. "He doesn't have to be frightened of Santa."

Huffman returned with Chris, who plopped down all his 400 plus pounds on the speechless Santa's lap.

The 1971 Midlands Tournament was next on the schedule for the Cyclones. Chris had rebounded from his fourth place finish in 1969 to capture his first Midlands crown in 1970. Wrestling unattached, he defeated Wojciechowski in the finals. Now, at the ninth annual meet in 1971, he was back as the defending champion — this time wearing the Cardinal and Gold of Iowa State. There wouldn't be a rematch with Wojciechowski, as he passed up the meet. But there was still plenty of stiff competition.

Chris charged to his second straight Midlands title in gaudy fashion. Michigan's rugged Big 10 champion Gary Ernst was pinned in 51 seconds in the first round, and Ron Bleck of Wisconsin-Superior lasted for five minutes and 59 seconds.

Victim number three was Chuck Jean, a two-time NCAA champion from Iowa State who was booted from ISU for his wild antics and who was competing for Adams State of Alamosa, Colorado. The irrepressible Jean, just a 177 pounder normally, had been out until 2 a.m. the day of the match drinking with friends. He waded straight into Chris, trying to lock his hands around the huge waist and secure his favorite hold, a bear hug. Taylor, grinning at Jean's audacity, hooked him under the arms and flung the scrappy wrestler to his back for a 55 second pin.

Mike McCready of rival Northern Iowa (now The University of Northern Iowa, located in Cedar Falls, Iowa), was the semifinal foe, and Chris worked hard to score a 4-0 victory over the powerful Panther. Mike Kelly of the Mayor Daley Youth Foundation became the third Taylor victim to go down in less than one minute. The 45 second pin gave Taylor a second title in America's toughest meet — and served official notice there was a new giant on the amateur wrestling scene!

Iowa State rolled up 86 points for its third team title as Chris tied former Iowa State great Dan Gable with four pins. Though Gable was awarded his fourth straight Outstanding Wrestling award, Chris won the Most Falls Trophy by pinning his foes in less time than Gable, by a margin of 7:00 to 15:33.

Two weeks later, a national-record crowd of 10,100 fans showed up at Ames to watch Iowa State and Oklahoma State battle it out on the mat in a dramatic dual meet. It was a typical ISU-OSU showdown, and the Cyclones trailed 15-12 going into the final two matches. But Peterson routed the Cowboys' Rick Jones 13-1 at 190 pounds, lifting ISU into a 16-15 lead setting the stage for an heroic climax.

During the Iowa State vs. Oklahoma State meet.

Chris delivered a crushing 48 second pin over Harry Geris, sending the hometown crowd into a roaring ovation. The 22-15 triumph was the 27th straight for the Cyclones.

The fast pin was becoming routine for the big guy, and so was the 40 minute autograph session. The name Chris Taylor had caught fire on the wrestling circuit and the autograph seekers formed lines that sometimes took over a half an hour to complete.

The workout partners — Peckham, Huffman, Peterson and former star Jim Duschen, a powerful 210 pounder — had also left their mark on Taylor. He was more aggressive than he had been in junior college.

"He's improved 100 percent since he's been here at Iowa State," said Gable, a graduate assistant at Iowa State after closing out his remarkable Cyclone career with a record of 117-1. "He used to be afraid to try things, but now he goes out there and gets after his foe."

The season was going great for Chris. He scored pins over Mankato State's Dennis Peirro in 5:22 as the Cyclones won 35-9. He received a forfeit in the Cyclones' 33-3 win over Navy. And he finished off Jim deVane in 3:35 in the Cyclones' 35-9 victory over Franklin and Marshall.

On January 15, the team traveled to Drake University in Des Moines, and shut out the Bulldogs 40-0. Don Bonner lasted just 1:56 in the final match.

"Look — Chris does two minutes of work on the mat, then signs autographs for an hour," said Nichols, shaking his head at the crowd gathered around his blossoming star.

The Cyclones continued to roll. In Fort Collins, Colorado, on January 19 the team won by a 46-9 margin over Colorado State, as Chris won again by forfeit. Continuing the road trip west, the Cyclones defeated Oregon State at Corvallis on January 21 by a score of 20-9. The Cyclones won their last five matches to pull out the win in a come-from-behind effort. Chris won a 7-2 decision over Jim Hagen, a scrappy 195 pounder who refused to give an inch even though he was outweighed by over 200 pounds.

Iowa State rode a 31-match winning streak into Seattle, Washington, to take on the University of Washington Huskies, an overnight mat power paced by the exciting style of Larry Owings. The Husky ticket department was unprepared for the dual attraction of the nation's top rated team and the gentle giant, and was overwhelmed by the size of the crowd. The afternoon meet was delayed by almost an hour, and a record 8,148 fans screamed wildly as their Huskies posted a startling 17-16 upset.

Photo courtesy of Ames Tribune

Chris remained undefeated with an 8-2 decision over Don Dunham, but was unable to pin the 235 pounder and score the extra two points that would have won the meet.

"I went out and gave it all I had," said a tired Dunham after the bout. "It's quite a feeling to have 400 pounds on top of you; yes, quite a feeling."

The trip home was a long one for the Cyclones. Traveling with Chris at his side on the airplane, Nichols and his team headed home to Ames.

When the team traveled on commercial planes, Chris sat in the coach section with the rest of the team. He never complained, even though the seats were very small and it was a tight and uncomfortable trip for him.

"Sometimes there would be room in the first class section where the seats are larger and the stewardess would ask Chris if he would want to move up; and he usually would, but he never complained," recalled Nichols years later.

When the team flew on the small Iowa State University airplanes they would split up, with five in one plane and six in the other. The plane carrying Chris would only hold five in order to balance the weight evenly.

"I could always find my wrestlers in the airports," said Nichols. "All I had to do was look for Chris, as he stood high above everyone else."

Fast on the heels of the Washington loss, Chris was about to suffer another "setback" in Ames. The ISU dual meets began at 7 p.m. and Lynne, feeling sorry for Chris since he lived in a motel, decided she should take care of the "poor guy" with nutritional meals. She rushed home from her job and cooked dinner before nearly every home dual.

The ritual began at the start of the season in November and continued for many weeks. Then, in January, Chris's grandparents traveled from Dowagiac to see him wrestle. After the meet, they took Lynne and Chris to dinner. During the conversation Chris described how after weigh-ins on Friday afternoons the team would go out to the Broiler, a supper club in Ames, for steak dinners.

"You mean to tell me that you have been going out for steak dinner — and then coming back to my place for another dinner as well?" asked Lynne. The meals at Lynne's apartment ended abruptly.

Lynne may have quit feeding Chris prior to the meets, but she didn't allow that small misunderstanding to in any way dampen her enthusiasm for his matches. She became a devoted Iowa State wrestling fan, writhing and twisting in her seat, grimacing and tugging on the coat sleeves of Huffman, who sat with her at most of the meets. Finally, Huffman began to ease away from her before Chris began to wrestle. If Chris worked hard on the mat, Lynne worked almost as hard in the stands, using her body english to "help" Chris, even though he seldom needed any sort of assistance at all.

The Cyclones rebounded from their first loss by dumping Lehigh 31-7 on January 28. Chris won by a pin over Mike D'Anjczek in 2:47 and signed autographs for 20 minutes before going to the showers.

But three days later in Norman, Oklahoma, Chris ran into an old foe and suffered what was to be the only blemish on his ISU record. Chris had scored a 3-1 decision over the Sooners' Bill Struve at the Southern Open back in the season opener, but was held to just one point in Norman. Struve scored first with a six second escape in the second period, and Chris tied it up with an escape 15 seconds into the final period. He had to settle for a 1-1 tie as the Cyclones rolled to a 28-10 triumph.

Chris rebounded with a pin over Todd Nicholson of Southern Illinois University on February 4 as the team won handily, 33-6. Shortly after, *Sports Illustrated*, the nation's premier sporting journal, showed up on his doorstep. Writer Herman Weiskopf explored the Taylor mystique in an article entitled "Very Big Man On Campus".

"As a wrestler, Taylor is surprisingly agile, has enormous strength and a knack for showmanship,' wrote Weiskopf. "When it is his turn to compete, he trots out to the mat amid booming cheers at home and rumbling boos away. At times, he thwarts an opponent's assault with a flick of his wrist or a shrug of his shoulder, much like a bull removing a fly with a swish of his tail."

He also touched on another side of the gentle giant, one that few others had noticed.

"Taylor's opponents are not the only ones who stand in awe of him. 'The fans are afraid of me, too,' he admits, a bit sadly. 'But then they see someone get an autograph from me and after that they come in bunches.' s"

It was a poignant moment, yet a common one for those destined to live their lives in physical realms that others can only gape at. Chris had grappled with his persona ever since birth, but had seldom articulated it.

Chris scored a 1:23 pin over Jerry Guth as the Cyclones humbled Wisconsin 38-3, and the next night the Cyclones hosted Cal Poly, sending them back to California with a 28-9 loss. Chris recorded another pin, this time in 1:47 over Keith Lelan, bringing his record for the year to 14-0-1.

In Boulder, Colorado, the Cyclones shut out the host Buffaloes 39-0. Chris handed Bill Kralicke a 6-4 loss, but again was pushed to his limit. Trailing 5-2, Kralicke scored a takedown with 25 seconds left in the match, closing the gap to 5-4. Chris couldn't escape, but was awarded a riding time point for a 6-4 victory.

Chris ready for a match, Les Anderson in the background.

The team ended the year with a 42-3 victory over the University of Wyoming at Laramie, Chris getting another forfeit. The Cyclones took a 16— record into the Big 8 Wrestling Championships at Stillwater, Oklahoma. They entered the tournament ranked number one in the nation and built an early lead. But Oklahoma State came from behind, and outscored Iowa State 92 to 85.50 to capture the title.

Chris, Rich Binek (177 pounds) and Peterson (190 pounds) all won championships. Chris pinned Colorado's Kralicek in 3:12 of

42nd NCAA Championships, in the front row are champions (l tor)Carl Adams, Chris and Ben Peterson. In the back row are (l to r) Zilverberg, Parker, Mallinger, Fjetland and Abens.

the first round to gain some measure of revenge for the tough battle the Buffalo had given him just two weeks earlier. In the semifinals he pinned Herris Butler of Missouri in 1:30 and in the finals he posted a 3-0 decision over Harry Geris of Oklahoma State.

Undefeated in 32 matches and with 24 pins (eight of which came in a minute or less), and just the one draw, Chris had one last hurdle.

The 42nd NCAA Wrestling Championships were at Color Field House at College Park, Maryland. Taylor opened with a pin in 2:50 over Larry Malinouski of Central Michigan University, and flattened Milton Seals of New Mexico in 4:41. Mike McCready, the nemesis from the University of Northern Iowa, extended Chris to the limit before dropping a hard-fought battle 2-0 match.

A 6-2 victory over Geris, of Oklahoma State, put Chris into the finals against the defending NCAA champion, Toledo's Greg Wojciechowski. The powerful 255 pounder had defeated Chris in the 1969 Midlands and Chris had defeated him in the 1970 Midlands finals. A year in the ISU room had made Chris much tougher, however, and despite jamming his left knee in an earlier round Chris posted a relatively easy 6-1 victory.

Joining him on the winners' stand were teammates Carl Adams (158 pounds) and Ben Peterson (190 pounds). The Cyclones scored their fifth team win, totaling 103 points to just 73.50 for runner-up Michigan State. Others scoring team points were Bill Fjetland (fifth at 126 pounds), Phil Parker (second at 134 pounds), Keith Abens (second at 167 pounds) and Rich Binek (third at 177 pounds).

Nichols decided to reward the team on a sight-seeing tour while so close to Washington, D.C. A trip was arranged to the United States Capital.

"I found it interesting that while we were in the Rotunda at the Capitol, this huge impressive room, it was Chris who was receiving all the attention," said Nichols. "Chris was just as much an attraction as the sights."

To this day, Nichols believes Chris was the greatest ambassador wrestling has ever had.

"He was big, outstanding, noticeable and personable to every-one," said Nichols. "He loved kids and they would stand in line waiting to get his autograph. During the meets when Chris wrestled, people would stay to the very end, just to see him wrestle. Most of the time they came to watch Chris and it didn't matter which team was ahead, they just wanted to see Chris wrestle."

The collegiate season had come to an end, but in April Chris was selected to wrestle on an American team which was hosting the Soviet National team. The Soviet team was touring the United States for a series of dual meets in conjunction with the World Cup Tournament held in Toledo, Ohio.

Chris's foe was the acknowledged star of the Soviet team, the legendary Alexander Medved, already a nine-time world champion. In a tour a year earlier, Medved had proven too much for the still inexperienced American, defeating Chris by scores of 3-0, 3-1 and 5-1. Yet, anticipation was at a fever pitch in wrestling circle for the rematch in 1972, which was scheduled to take place at McElroy Auditorium in Waterloo, Iowa. The crowd of 5,000 in Dan Gable's hometown were disappointed, however, as Medved elected not to wrestle citing an injury. The two exchanged gifts, but the wrestling community would not see them collide until the 1972 Olympics...in a titanic battle no fan would ever forget!

That spring, the City of Dowagiac presented Chris with a procla-mation citing him for his achievements in wrestling and for spread-ing the name of the city throughout the nation and the world. They called Chris a "goodwill ambassador" for Dowagiac.

He and former Union High School star, Vern Davis, were hon-

Photo by Dan Jacob, 1971, Waterloo Courier

Chris's foe was the acknowledged star of the Soviet team, the legendary Alexander Medved, already a nine-time world champion.

ored at a banquet at the high school. Both were former city athletes who had gone on to national prominence in the sports field, Chris as an NCAA champion and Davis as a defensive safety for the Philadelphia Eagles in the National Football League. Chris used the occasion to outline his goals for the near future.

"I'm going back to Iowa tomorrow and begin working out again." Chris told the gathering. "I have three fellows who weigh about 300 pounds each and they said that they would work out with me. I will try out for the United States Olympic wrestling team this summer. I am working very hard for the chance to meet Alexander Medved. He's beaten me the three times we have faced each other and I want a chance to get back at him."

1972 Oylmpic Trials
Anoka, Minnesota

CHAPTER 6
1972 Olympic Trials

Preparations for the Summer Olympics of 1972 really began for most wrestlers at the moment their collegiate seasons finished in March. However, the postgraduate athletes, veterans like Rick Sanders and Don Behm, had been training with the Olympic games uppermost in their minds for several years.

The road to a berth on the 1972 Olympic wrestling team officially got under way with regional trails in April all across the nation. Chris entered the regional in Iowa City, home of the University of Iowa, and won...but not without a scare. An unknown from Clinton, Iowa, Dick Taylor, who weighed in over the 300 pound mark, came within an eyelash of pinning Chris in an early match. The Clinton

Courtesy of Hills Studio, Ames, IA

Chris in his Olympic dress uniform, which was worn in the opening ceremonies in Munich's 1972 Olympic Games.

Taylor caught the Dowagiac Taylor in a lateral drop, throwing him hugely to the mat, flat on his back. The crowd erupted as Chris rolled to his stomach, barely escaping the pin. He fought back for a pin over the upstart from Clinton, and then won four more matches and the regional championship.

In May, the qualifiers from the eight regional tournaments converged on Anoka, Minnesota, a suburb of Minneapolis, for the final trials. Lynne rode up from Ames with Chris to the trials, where they arrived late for the weigh-ins. They were stopped for speeding along the way, but the officer let them go when Chris explained where they were headed, and how late they were.

"I left Chris off and then returned to the wrestling arena some-time later in the day," said Lynne. "I entered the arena and saw Chris and, like always, there was a large crowd of people around him. He saw me and we waved to each other and I noticed he was laughing."

Later Lynne asked him, "Why were you laughing when I came into the arena?"

"Those guys I was standing with asked me what my girlfriend looks like," said Chris. "I told them you were six foot seven inches tall and had one eye right in the middle of your forehead.

"When you came in I said to the guys, 'There she is now' and they said, 'No, that can't be', and we all had a laugh."

Chris maintained his jovial mood throughout most of the trials. Ron Maley, a sportswriter with the *Des Moines Register*, painted a picture of contrasts between the approaches of Taylor and the incredibly intense Gable.

" 'I'm a pretty easygoing guy," said Taylor. 'I've always been that way. Why? I guess because my parents told me they wanted me to be a good boy.'

"Taylor's preparations for a match are in direct contrast to those of Dan Gable, the brilliant 149.5 pound former Iowa State wrestler," wrote Maley. "Gable is unsmiling and hard to find between matches. If he isn't wrestling, he's thinking about it or he's running. There is never a wasted moment.

" 'I never find a lot of things to get uptight about,' Taylor commented. 'I might be happy-go-lucky beforehand, but I can get serious when I'm ready to wrestle. I do get psyched up for a match just before I go onto a mat.' "

Chris pinned his first four foes with relative ease, then ran into Mike McCready, the former Northern Iowa star. The two battled fiercely, no quarter asked and none given, until McCready was disqualified in the final period for stalling.

"It should have been a double disqualification," McCready said as he stormed off the mat. "Taylor wasn't doing anything either.

"Besides, he was stepping on my foot — and that's against the rules."

It was the second meeting of the two in less than three months. Chris had edged McCready 2-0 in the NCAA meet, in which McCready wound up third. After the NCAA meet, Chris called McCready his toughest foe, and he echoed his respect for the 230 pounder after the Anoka match.

"I was going after him," said Chris. "He's a tough man for his size. He's very tough to pin."

In the finals, Chris found himself pitted against another old adversary, Greg Wojciechowski of Toledo. It was Wojciechowski who had beaten Chris in the 1969 Midlands, and it was Wojciechowski Chris had beaten in the finals of the 1970 Midlands...and the finals of the 1972 NCAA Tournament. The two knew one another's mat style very well.

Chris prevailed, 5-1, and found himself on the United States freestyle Olympic team, along with former Iowa State stars Gable (149.5) and Ben Peterson (198). Other members of the freestyle team were Sergio Gonzales at 105.5, 17 year-old Jimmy Carr at 114.5, Rick Saunders at 125.5, Gene Davis at 136.5, Wayne Wells at 163, John Peterson (brother of Ben) at 180.5 and Henk Schenk at 220.

But there wasn't time to rest just yet. Chris decided to try a very rare double; he wanted to represent the United States in both styles of wrestling — freestyle and Greco-Roman.

Freestyle wrestling had been popular in the United States since the turn of the century. Its wide open, almost anything goes style was very suitable to the American psyche. Greco-Roman, however, was considered too restrictive by most American matmen. It was a style that allowed no holds below the waist, and placed a heavy emphasis on chest-to-chest pummeling, and tremendous upper body conditioning. It is extremely popular in the Scandinavian countries and the Soviet Bloc nations. By 1972, there were an estimated 10,000 Greco-Roman wrestlers in then Soviet Union, compared to a mere 200 in the United States.

Chris breezed through the Greco-Roman trials, putting his tremendous weight advantage to good use. Again, it was Chris and Wojciechowski in the finals. Their first match ended in a tie, but Chris scored a pin in eight minutes and 50 seconds of the second bout to get his "double".

Another former Cyclone, Bob Buzzard, made the team at 149.5 pounds, giving Iowa State five of the twenty berths on the two teams. In addition, Jim Duschen narrowly missed making the Greco-Roman team at 220 pounds.

The trails in Anoka played an extremely instrumental role in Chris's life, allowing him the opportunity to make the Olympic teams and to subsequently gain world wide renown in the Summer Games. He was the largest man ever to compete in the Olympic Games in wrestling.

But the trials were important for another reason. They provided his introduction to a man who would eventually open the door for Chris in yet another profession.

"I saw Chris for the first time when he wrestled against the Soviets earlier in the year, in Anoka," said Verne Gagne, in 1988. "After the Olympic trials, I invited the entire team, with coaches and trainers, to my house for a barbecue. I remember telling Chris at the time he could have a career in professional wrestling, and for him to look me up when his amateur career was over."

Gagne, a former two time NCAA champion at the University of Minnesota, was an Olympic alternate to the great Henry Wittenberg in 1948. He made the trip to London and watched as Wittenberg captured the gold medal in the 198 pound class. Gagne then returned to America and began one of the most successful professional wrestling careers of all time. By 1972, he was also involved in promoting the sport, and had a stable of wrestlers he helped find matches for.

Lynne had stayed through the trials and Chris rode back to Iowa with her. They managed to squeeze in a quick trip to Dowagiac to visit Chris's family, and were home in Ames for a brief period before Chris returned to Anoka for the final Olympic training camp.

"I think at that point, he was ready to wrestle and to get rid of me for a while," she recalled.

The two Olympic teams, along with most of the alternates, spent one more month at camp. The camp was intense and demanding; the coaches — Bill Farrell in freestyle and Alan Rice in Greco-Roman often put two men on Chris at the same time. They wanted him in the best possible shape for the gruelling period that lay ahead. Not only did he need to learn the freestyle scoring system, substantially different from American college rules, but he also needed to concentrate on the various subtleties of international competition...not only in freestyle, but in Greco-Roman as well. As the only American competing in both styles, he faced a double burden.

Lynne drove to Anoka on weekends to see him, providing Chris with a break from wrestling that he needed. The two spent time driving around the city and seeing movies, but were mainly concerned with just spending time together. Lynne was saddened about the impending separation; the team was going to be in Munich for a lengthy time before the wrestling actually began, in order to allow for the adjustment of the different time zone and jet lag. Both Chris and Lynne knew the separation would be long, and painful.

The actual Olympic trip began with a flight from Minneapolis to Washington, D.C., where the wrestlers were to pick up their Olympic uniforms. While in the nation's capital, the team was invited to an August 17 dinner held by the President's Council on Physical Fitness and Sports. The dinner was held in the Persian Room at the Marriott Hotel and team members were requested to wear their Olympic travel uniforms.

Throughout his life, when Chris needed new clothes, a major shopping crisis resulted. At 430 pounds, he was six foot five inches tall, and wore a size 58 long jacket. His measurements included a 22 inch neck, a 52 inch waist and a 60 inch chest. He wore a size 15EEE shoe. His mother was always altering clothes to make them fit – but admitted there was little she could do with the shoe situation.

The Sears, Roebuck and Company tailor in Washington, D.C. was in charge of fitting Chris's uniform, and was faced with the challenge of his career. The final product fit Chris well, however, and he was finally set for Munich.

The grandest sports spectacle on the face of the earth was set to begin...and Chris Taylor was about to be introduced to the entire world.

U.S. News Service photo

Chris being fitted for his Olympic coat and uniform.

The 1972 Olympic Uniform

CHAPTER 7
Meeting Alexander Medved

No one who witnessed the Olympic Games of 1972 in Munich is likely to ever forget them. The German people had last hosted the world's most spectacular athletic event in Berlin, in 1936. Despite the awesome splendor of the 1936 Games, where the German Reich had spared no expense to showcase what it had imagined was a superior race and lifestyle, the Berlin Olympics have been forever associated with the tyranny of Adolph Hitler, who shortly after plunged the world into the greatest global conflict yet seen.

The West German Republic was determined to make the 1972 Olympics an event without flaw, and to erase the memory of the Hitler Games. A record 122 nations participated in Munich, bringing a record 7,147 athletes. A staggering sum was spent, including $62 million alone for the enormous acrylic canopy which covered much of the site.

The opening ceremonies of any Olympics are always a resplendent affair, and the 150,000 spectators jammed into Olympic Stadium in Munich roared their approval as the athletes marched in. The Greeks in the parade symbolized the fact their land was the birthplace of the original Olympics nearly 1,000 years before Christ. The costumes were designed as a means of identification for each country; the Cubans wore red berets, the Indians black turbans, the Irish were bedecked in green and the Bermudians sported Bermuda shorts.

The parade of athletes lasted nearly 90 minutes, and was accompanied by a group of 3,000 Munich school children who offered bouquets and wreaths of flowers to the athletes. Some 5,000 doves were set free, cannons blasted their salutes and the Olympic torch was brought in by the very last of 5,976 runners. It had been carried a distance of 5,539 kilometers in 29 days and seven hours.

The United States athletes marched into the stadium as the Star Spangled Banner blared. The most conspicuous was Chris Taylor, the largest athlete ever to compete in the modern Olympic games.

The competition was marked by the incredible performances of American swimmer Mark Spitz, who captured seven gold medals; by the Soviet Union's impish gymnast Olga Korbut, who smiled and flipped her way into the hearts of millions of fans; by Cuba's awesome boxer Teofilo Stevenson, who captured the first of three gold medals in the heavyweight division, and by American wrestler Dan Gable, who breezed to the gold medal at 149.5 pounds without surrendering a single point in six matches.

But there was more to the Munich Games. Much more. In the murky dawn of September 5, eight members of the Black September terrorist group entered the Israeli compound unnoticed. Before the horror had played itself out, 11 Israeli athletes had been murdered in a senseless and brutal act of atrocity. The world watched numbly on television; the memories of Munich left deep scars on millions.

"My unforgettable experience from Munich was the Israeli massacre," Ben Peterson, a gold medal wrestling champion at 198 pounds, said nearly two decades later. Quoted in the book, *Tales of Gold*, Peterson expounded:

"Everything was so nice in the Village. There we were, athletes from all over the world. We could shake hands, talk to one another through interpreters and exchange gifts. So I began to think that maybe all that I'd heard about the problems of the world weren't true. I thought that maybe there could be peace on earth. Maybe man could find his own solutions, and just maybe, sports should lead the way."

It was an idealistic view, shared by many Olympians, and shattered in the dawn of Munich. The hope expressed by Peterson was dealt another crushing blow eight years later when President Jimmy Carter decided the United States would boycott the Olympic Games in Moscow.

The freestyle wrestling competition in Munich had ended prior to the terrorism. The team, coached by Bill Farrell, turned in its finest performance in decades, returning to America with a total of six medals. Gable, Peterson and Wayne Wells (163 pounds) all won gold medals, while Rick Sanders (125.5 pounds) and John Peterson (180.5) claimed silvers. But the biggest story centered around the bronze medal that went to Taylor.

Alexander Medved is arguably the most successful amateur wrestler of all time. With ten world championships to his credit (seven at the World Games and three in the Olympic Games), he owns the most world titles of any wrestler.

Born September 16, 1937, he grew to manhood in the small Ukrainian town of Belaya Tserkov, where his father toiled as a forest ranger. He wrestled informally as a youngster, but didn't officially take up the sport until joining the army at the age of 20. As a young recruit, he was singled out by an officer for a training session. It proved to be a dark moment for the officer, and a bright day for

Soviet wrestling. Medved dominated his far more experienced partner in the training sessions and sembarked upon his own mat career.

In 15 international competitions, Medved lost just two of his 73 bouts. According to the official international wrestling press guide, "Medved's foremost qualities were technical virtuosity, excellent physical fitness, an enormous willpower, and a capacity of 100 percent concentration at the crucial moments."

Medved owned a 3-0 edge over the American giant when they collided in Munich. The Soviet superstar had scored 3-0, 3-1 and 5-1 victories of Taylor in a series of dual meets in the United States the year prior, and was vastly more experienced in the international wars. At six foot seven, he enjoyed a two-inch height advantage over Taylor. He was able to exploit his leverage advantage and his "enormous willpower" just enough to offset the American's 140 pound weight advantage.

The wrestling competition was held in a rather bland arena, with mats situated on a platform nearly six feet above the main floor, allowing the spectators a tremendous view of the action. Among the large crowd were many Americans, including the parents of most of the wrestlers and Dr. Harold Nichols, who had the honor of watching three of his former pupils (Gable, Peterson and Taylor) compete.

Working from a blind draw, Medved and Taylor were paired in the very first match of the heavyweight competition. The two matmen from opposite sides of the world circled warily for most the nine minute match, Medved feinting sporadically and Taylor wading in, trying to force a tie-up, from where he could perhaps put his weight advantage to work.

The referee, Umit Demirag of Turkey, in an effort to speed up the action awarded caution points to each men on two separate occasions, despite the fact it appeared to most observers that the American was forcing action on the mat. That made the score 2-2. Then near the end of the match, Medved demonstrated the tremendous concentration and willpower he was famous for.

Executing a courageous arm drag single leg trip maneuver, the Soviet shot in on Taylor and tripped him to the mat for a one point takedown, and a 3-2 lead. The crowd erupted in an avalanche of noise, then quieted as Taylor tried gamely to score a takedown in the waning seconds. When time expired, Medved sank to the mat and kissed it in a symbolic farewell gesture. He had defeated his gigantic American foe, and was retiring from the sport.

Controversy raged over the referee's assessing points against each wrestler, most fans feeling Taylor had been far more aggressive than Medved and should not have been penalized. When Demirag admitted he had felt obligated to penalize Taylor because he out-weighed the Soviet, a howl of protest went up, and Demirag was banned from further officiating the remainder of the tourney.

"Chris Taylor's first round, much disputed loss to Medved was the talk of the tournament," wrote Farrell shortly after the Games. "Everyone except a confused referee and mat judge was convinced that Medved was guilty of passivity. The referee, later dismissed, stated Taylor weighed twice as much as Medved; thus, he did not caution the Russian. No doubt Medved's illustrious record influenced these confused officials."

Though he had never beaten Medved, Taylor carried an optimistic attitude into the 1972 Olympics. He had been seen in the Olympic Village wearing a tee shirt that proclaimed, "Yea, though I walk through the valley of the shadow of death I will fear no evil, for I'm the meanest SOB in the valley."

The shirt's message was not typical Taylor, as he was no braggart. It was, however, evidence that he was trying to prepare himself mentally and emotionally for what would prove to be the most important bout of his long career.

"If Chris had been wrestling anyone but Alexander Medved, he would have won the match on cautions and been the Olympic heavyweight champion," wrote Wayne Baughman in his book, *On and Off the Mat*. Baughman was a member of the 1972 Greco-Roman team, and served as head coach for the 1976 Olympic freestyle team in Montreal.

Gable agreed with both Farrell and Baughman that Taylor was the aggressor in the match, and that he probably should have won the bout on caution points. And yet, he points to a fact that many have overlooked.

"Medved was definitely stalling," said Gable, who would go on from his Olympic triumph to coach the 1980 and 1984 Olympic teams, and defeat the Soviets twice as coach of World Cup teams. "But, it was hard to call it on him, I guess, because the fact of the matter is Medved did have the only scoring move of the match, that arm drag trip. Because of that one technical point he scored, it was hard to call him for stalling."

The Taylor-Medved flap wasn't the only major controversy that sprouted up between the two superpowers in Munich. The gold medal in basketball went to the Soviet Union in a tremendous upset, and the American team was so angered that it refused to accept the silver medals for second place. The dispute erupted over confusion at the end of the game. The United States held a 50-49 lead with three seconds left on the clock. A series of bizarre events transpired and, against all logic, the Soviets wound up with a 51-50 victory. Several protests by the United States were to no avail.

Taylor, though greatly disappointed by the setback against Medved, scored four more victories to earn the bronze medal. He decisioned Bulgaria's Osman Douraliev, but the Bulgarian finished ahead of him in second place under the international style of ranking.

Unlike the basketball players, Taylor was proud of his medal, and accepted the bronze graciously. Several months later, while competing at the Bison Open Tournament in Fargo, North Dakota, he also spoke of his respect for Medved.

"I met him in the first round and that was okay with me," Taylor told local sports editor Ed Kolpack. "I figured I might as well find out right now how good I am. In the first two rounds I had him on the run; he didn't take two steps forward. I was getting tired of chasing him. In the last round, he came on stronger. He was smart."

A year after Munich, while honeymooning in Boise, Idaho, the Gentle Giant offered yet another, very candid appraisal of his match with Medved.

"If I'd gone out and wrestled the guy the way that I should have, there would have been no doubt in anybody's mind whether I won or lost," he told *Boise Statesman* sportswriter Jim Poore. "As it was, I knew I got beat. I didn't go out and push hard enough. You might say I was scared of him a little bit; he had been world champion seven times."

Taylor had a chance to redeem himself in the Greco-Roman competition which followed the freestyle event. Greco-Roman is a style which limited wrestling to holds above the waist, and which disallowed all use of the legs. It had surfaced in the late 1800s in Europe, where it was perceived as the true classical form of wrestling preferred by the Greeks. It is nowhere near as popular in the United States as it is in Europe, and the Soviet Bloc countries.

His first match was against the East German champion Wilfred Dietrich, who had finished fifth in freestyle. Chris had scored a decision over Dietrich in freestyle, but Dietrich, like Medved, was a wise and seasoned veteran of international events. He won the Olympics in 1960 and the world meet in 1961, and was also a judo champion, capable of big, explosive moves.

Prior to the Olympics, Dietrich had met the American Giant in a practice session. Sauntering over with a friendly smile, Dietrich teasingly attempted to wrap his arms around Taylor; what seemed like a good natured gesture was in all probability an attempt to assess whether or not he could lock his hands behind Taylor's back.

In the Greco-Roman match in Munich, Dietrich waded into the American and once again wrapped his arms around Taylor's massive chest. Dietrich then locked his hands...initiated an incredibly daring move. The resulting throw, and the photo showing it, have entered into wrestling folklore.

There in the photo, for the world to see, is Dietrich facing the camera in the midst of a bear hug, his teeth gritted as he heads for the mat, Chris Taylor riding on top of him. To the uninitiated, it appears as though Taylor is enroute to an easy pin, needing only to fall on his West German foe. But to those familiar with the techniques of international wrestling, they realize Taylor is in the midst of being thrown in a move known as a soufflé.

Dietrich hit the mat, landing on his head, his incredibly powerful neck absorbing the impact of Taylor's bulk. In far less time than it takes to explain it, Dietrich executed a lightning-quick spin, turning Taylor underneath him. The perfectly executed soufflé was completed; the American giant was flat on his back beneath Dietrich, the victim of a stunning pin!

Dietrich had tried the move on Taylor in the freestyle portion, but hadn't been successful. Baughman, who finished his career with 16 national titles, many coming in Greco-Roman, had warned Taylor of Dietrich's big throw prior to their match.

"Chris, like most Americans, preferred an overhook to an underhook (in the tie-up position)," said Baughman. "I had been telling him that he had to control the underhook, especially against this guy. I had seen films of Dietrich in the 1961 World Championships throwing 350 pound Hallow Wilson with three straight belly-to-back soufflés, so I knew he could throw.

"Chris went out and was pretty well pushing Dietrich around in the first period, but it was obvious Dietrich was trying to set up his throw. Between periods I yelled at Chris from the sidelines to control the underhook and to watch Dietrich positioning for a throw.

"Chris went straight out and locked a double overhook and the German took off. It was a desperate effort for Dietrich that paid off big. Dietrich knew he couldn't stay with Chris much longer and took advantage of the opportunity when it arrived. He must have sunk a foot into the mat when they hit, but he had the momentum to keep going and came out on top for the fall."

Baughman and several other observers felt Dietrich could have been called for a fall himself at the moment he landed. Twice in the same Olympics, the Dowagiac matman had come out on the losing end of extremely close calls.

"Later I went back to our dressing area and Chris was sitting on a training table swinging his legs and looking like a giant little kid," added Baughman. "He looked up at me and said, 'Well, you told me so. I really didn't believe there was anybody in the world who could lift me off the mat and throw me, but I was wrong.' "

In his second Greco-Roman match, against 1968 Olympic bronze medalist Pat Kment of Czechoslovakia, both Taylor and Kment were disqualified for passivity. Suddenly, the wrestling portion of the 1972 Olympics was history. The largest person ever to compete in the history of the Games had won four matches and lost three, two of the losses coming in spectacular, if not perplexing fashion.

The Olympics had been a family experience for many Americans, including the Taylors. His parents and sisters were sent to Germany through the courtesy of Dowagiac citizens.

"We hadn't planned on making the trip since we had just moved into our new home and we didn't have the extra money to be flying off to Germany," said Jim, "even as much as we really wanted to go. I had used all my vacation time and money to make this home possible.

"The trip absolutely would not have been possible but for the kindness of those who contributed to make a dream come true for us."

Dowagiac businessmen chipped in to pay for the flights of Jim and Vera, and the grandparents paid the way for Sherrie and Becky (17 and 13, respectively). It was the first trip out of the country for the entire Taylor family, who were housed with a German family in the small town of Unterammergau, some 70 miles south of Munich. The Taylors stayed with the Joseph Karlwein family, and spent 22 days there. They took the train to Munich each day, a trip of 90 minutes each way.

The town was a scenic wonder, nestled in the foothills of the Alps. Most of the homes were made of thick cement, with barns connected to the backs of the houses. The houses are kept in the same family for generations, handed down from parents to children time after time.

Each morning, the cows were led from the barns to the mountain pastures to graze, and then brought back at dusk. Though there wasn't a single car in the village, there was at least one tractor...with several seats on it so that the owner could take riders with him up to where the cows and horses were grazing.

All accommodations for the families of the wrestlers were arranged by the United States Wrestling Federation. Just one girl in the entire village was able to speak much English, and was kept busy as an interpreter. Still, communication wasn't much of a problem, due to the ability of both the hosts and guests to express themselves through gestures and facial expressions.

Chris visited his family in Unterammergau between the freestyle and Greco-Roman competition, and upon arriving by train was an immediate attraction. He was followed down the streets by groups of children who shouted out his name, and the 91 year-old town priest made a special trip to the Karlwein home just to see the Gentle Giant from the United States.

Even the town yodelers put in a special appearance. They came dressed in short leather pants and fancy vests, with feathers in their hats. Joseph Karlwein and his sister played their accordions and the yodelers performed into the night. There are no age limits for beer drinking in Germany, and the youngsters joined in the merriment right alongside the adults, drinking and dancing for hours.

When Chris returned to the Olympic Village, it was the night before the terrorists' dawn attack. The Israeli quarters were only several buildings away from where the American wrestlers were housed, and Farrell and Gable actually walked past the general area of the attack on their way back to the track stadium as police and army vehicles were moving into place. However, no information was being dispensed, and most of the athletes and coaches were unaware of the gravity of the situation until later.

Eventually, the Olympic Village was sealed off. In the central plaza, athletes carried on as though nothing was amiss. Some played ping pong, others played miniature golf; in a building less than 100 yards away a volleyball game was in progress.

"We could see people crowding all around, but we couldn't go down where the attack was taking place," said Chris. "I heard the shots early in the morning, but didn't realize what was going on or how close it actually was to me. I wasn't in a hurry to get near the shooting; I make too big a target."

At the same time, the Taylor family was struggling to pick up bits and pieces of what was transpiring.

"We couldn't go in to see Chris wrestle, but we couldn't understand why," said Sherrie. "All we knew was that something bad had happened; we just didn't have any communication."

Jim recalled years later that they were all confused until some-one gave them a note, "and we were shocked and scared for the athletes."

Eventually, as word of the attack leaked out, the mood changed dramatically in the village. It quickly became somber as the athletes pondered the brutality of the act.

"When the deaths were announced, the United States athletes were confused at first, then dejected," said Farrell years later. "As you can expect the major question was...should the Games go on? Most athletes felt they should."

On September 6, the morning after the killings had taken place, nearly 80,000 gathered in Olympic Stadium to mourn the slain Israe-lis. The flags of the 122 competing nations flew at half mast. Munich's Philharmonic orchestra played Beethoven music, and West Germany President Gustav Heinemann sadly declared, "We stand helpless before a truly despicable act."

The drama ended in a blaze of gunfire at the airport where the eight Arab terrorists had flown by helicopters with their nine Israeli hostages. When it was over, the nine hostages were killed, bringing the Israeli death toll to 11, and five of the eight terrorists were also gunned down.

The Olympic movement changed in Munich. Security precau-tions marked the Games in 1976, where over $100 million was spent to ensure the safety of the athletes in Montreal. And life also changed for the athletes. Medved returned to a hero's welcome in the Soviet Union. While wrestling was a sporting activity for Americans, it was an occupation for the Soviets. The government completely subsidizes its top athletes, providing them with a home and financial support while they train to earn glory for their country.

In 1974, Medved was honored at a retirement party at the Sports Palace in Minsh. An estimated 6,000 fans were on hand to show their respect and affection, and to review his great career, which included such decorations as The Order of Lenin, The Order of the Red Ban-ner of Labor and The Order of the Badge of Honor. He entered into the life of an engineer, and years later was seen occasionally officiat-ing at important meets.

For Chris Taylor, it was back to school. It was a long way from Munich, Germany, to Ames, Iowa, in many ways. But Chris still had his senior year at Iowa State to complete.

It was destined to be a year of gigantic achievements.

John Peterson, Ben Peterson, Wayne Wells, Dan Gable, Chris Taylor, and Rick Saunders, the 1972 Olymians.

The Gentle Giant

CHAPTER 8
Coming Home With a Bronze Medal

While Chris and his family were in Munich, caught up in the incredible excitement — and then the staggering horror — of the 1972 Olympics, Lynne remained in Ames. She continued working at Younkers Department Store, and each day she arrived at work she would find news articles about Chris laying at her work area.

"I felt left out, everyone had gone to Munich," she said. "I was happy that Chris's family was able to go. Huffy and I watched the opening ceremonies but when it was time for Chris to wrestle, wouldn't you know it, the match was preempted

Jim Taylor (L) Chris on Right with Taylor family host in Germany during the 1972 Olympics.

for a baseball game; and I can tell you the people in Ames were really upset."

Lynne's fellow workers at Younkers did their part to help Lynne watch Chris wrestle. Televisions all over the store were turned to the Olympics. Workers all around the store shouted with excitement when Chris wrestled, and she was able to share her joy with her friends at work.

When the competition in Munich finally ended, the honors and recognitions were just beginning. A host of telegrams poured into the Olympic Village, before the competition, as well as after.

"Chris, you make us proud, give'em heck," wrote the Dowagiac Jaycees.

"Congratulations on success, we're pulling for you, God Bless," wrote the Muskegon Community College Faculty Association.

James Burke, mayor of Dowagiac, sent the longest telegram: "On behalf of the citizens of the City of Dowagiac, we would like to wish you the best of luck in the upcoming Olympic event in which you will be participating. The entire city of Dowagiac will be listening to the radio and watching their televisions to share in the many victories we are sure you will accomplish. At the regular council meeting of August 7, 1972, the council acted on a proclamation wishing you the best of luck at the Olympics representing the United States."

After the Olympics, it was more of the same.

"Congratulations from the City of Ames, Iowa, on your bronze medal at the Olympics," wrote Stuart Smith, mayor of Ames.

A letter from the White House, from President Richard Nixon, also arrived.

"All of America joins me in welcoming you home from the 1972 Summer Olympics. Your bronze medal in the super heavyweight class is a splendid tribute not only to your skill as an athlete but perhaps more importantly to your dedication to the ideas of the Olympic tradition. On behalf of your fellow citizens, I am delighted to extend my heartiest congratulations to you for the honor you have brought to yourself and to your community."

Chris slipped into Dowagiac with very few knowing of his return. Lynne picked him up at the airport in South Bend, Indiana, and they drove to the Taylor home, where Chris's grandparents were staying.

Photo Courtesy of ISU Sports Information

Chris, Gable and Peterson were honored at half-time of an Iowa State football game.

The Gentle Giant

He was home for a day and a half before the news of his return spread through town. Members of *The Dowagiac Daily News* staff arrived at the farm for a story, and snapped photos of Lynne holding Chris's bronze medal hanging from the ribbon around his neck. The First National Bank proudly displayed "Congratulations Chris Taylor" across its front. And the Cass County Board of Commissioners designated September as "Chris Taylor Month" in the county where Dowagiac is located.

But he wasn't able to stay and savor the appreciation that surely would have been heaped upon him as the town's first Olympian and most famous citizen. Classes had already started at Iowa State, and he was soon on his way back to Cyclone country.

Chris, Gable and Peterson were honored at half-time of an Iowa State football game and received a standing ovation from the large crowd. In recognition of his huge impact on the sport, Chris finished third in the balloting for "Man of the Year", wrestling's most prestigious award. It was a highly unusual honor for a college athlete, as the award almost always goes to men who have moved far beyond their collegiate days. Farrell finished first, while Peterson was second. Since previous winners were not eligible, Gable was not on the list.

Of course, the appreciation that was showered upon Chris was a two-way street for the Taylor family. They were all grateful for the kindness shown them, and Jim and Vera responded with a letter which appeared in *The Dowagiac Daily News*.

"How do you say thanks so very much to each individual who was so generous in making our trip to Munich possible? We sincerely feel indebted to the city and hope we can do a little to help someone else.

"It was sincerely a wonderful feeling for us to see Chris at the podium accepting his bronze medallion and the American flag being raised at the other end of the wrestling stadium in his honor. All of us were rather stunned and humbled watching each of the awards, with the thought that these were representatives of the world. The feeling of each with the opportunity to represent his country, the feeling he was a part of this, and each one, winner or not, hoping that everyone back home felt he had done a good job.

"Thanks so much for this opportunity."

In October of 1972 Chris was honored by the Michigan State Legislature in the form of a resolution. He had carried the banner of his hometown and his state — not only with his outstanding athletic ability, but also his warm, friendly manner — and his Olympic saga was voted Dowagiac's top news story of 1972.

But perhaps the biggest honor of all came in a personal letter to Chris from coach Bill Farrell.

"It is truly rewarding to return to the United States to find that wrestling was the hottest item on television and to find all sports fans in this country, not just wrestling fans, talking about our team," wrote Farrell. "I hope that you are aware of the great contributions you personally have made toward making wrestling so popular.

"Chris, I actually wanted to comment on your cooperation and attitude during the training camp and competition. Except for a few times when we did not see eye to eye on practices, you were very cooperative and a great asset to the team. Earlier in the camp I was not aware that you were such a hard worker but after I realized that you would never shirk your responsibilities as a member of the team, there was no problem. I wish that every team member had your attitude."

Back in Ames, with the euphoria of the Olympics fast receding, Chris began experiencing feelings of frustration about wrestling. It was brought on by a combination of factors. There was the letdown after a great first year at Iowa State, the disappointment of the loss to Medved, and then returning to school after classes had already begun.

Lynne was also feeling left out of Chris's life. He had grown extremely popular in the past few months, and she felt somewhat excluded. In late November, by the time Thanksgiving arrived, Lynne had nearly decided to give up on her relationship with Chris.

"It almost ended for us," she confided in 1988. "I thought about leaving Iowa and returning to Michigan for good. Then Chris started talking about marriage. In fact, that's all he talked about for two whole days."

A formal marriage proposal never happened, but they announced wedding plans to their families at Christmas. The wedding date was set for September 8. First, however, another year of wrestling at Iowa State was about to unfold. And before wrestling began, there was...football.

Chris enjoyed his high school football experiences, and often talked about going out for the Iowa State football team. When the Iowa media got wind of his plans, it became an intriguing news item, from one end of the state to the other.

ISU Coach Johnny Majors publicly gave his blessing, though he seemed reserved: "We're glad to have him out," said Majors, quickly adding, "I will not answer any questions simply because the average fan knows as much about it as I do."

Chris showed up at an early season practice wearing football practice pants and cleats. *The Associated Press* moved photos of him on their wire machines, and one cutline under a photo, which showed Chris bending over said, "Even at 400 plus pounds, Taylor can bend over and reach the grass."

The experiment was short lived, though. The Cyclone athletic department simply couldn't come up with suitable equipment of an adequate size, and Chris soon was forced to abandon the dream.

"I really wanted to play, but they didn't have a lid (helmet) big enough for me," Chris said.

He had hoped the football experience would complement his wrestling. Chris knew he needed to stay active in order to control his weight, and he felt football would help keep him in condition for wrestling. Otherwise, all the off season offered in the way of conditioning was a weight program, and he found weight lifting of little interest.

Chris opened the wrestling season at the annual Bison Open, held at North Dakota State University in Fargo. He was coaxed into entering the meet by his friend, Jim Duschen, who had left ISU and was working on his masters' degree at North Dakota State.

Prior to the meet, a friend at Iowa State asked Chris where he was wrestling on Saturday.

"I'm going to the Bison Open in Fargo, North Dakota," he said.

"What is the Bison Open?" the friend inquired.

"That's where you wrestle buffalo," he deadpanned.

Hardly anyone could blame any of the other heavyweights in the Bison Open field if they felt they were indeed matched against a buffalo when facing the giant Cyclone. The combination of confidence gained from his NCAA title, experience gained from the Olympics, and the continued physical maturity was molding Chris Taylor into what many would come to regard as the finest heavyweight in collegiate history.

"I realized what I was getting myself into when I asked him to come up," said Duschen, from Henderson, Nevada where he fashioned a very successful program at Basic High School. "I entered the tournament, too, and I knew there was a good chance we would end up wrestling each other. But I also knew it would be great for the sport in North Dakota, for those fans to get to see Chris in person, right after the Olympics."

Taylor and Duschen, who weighed 215 at the time, both made the finals, and Chris scored a pin in 1:55 of the first period.

"I didn't know any other way to wrestle than to just go right in," said Duschen. "I went in and underhooked him; he countered me, we went to the mat, and I thought a ton of bricks had come down on me. I got away, and we got right back in the same position. We went down on the mat, and when I stood up, he came up with me, and lifted. I thought I was going right through the roof. I remember thinking, 'What am I doing here?' "

An extremely powerful man himself, Duschen was overwhelmed by the combination of Taylor's weight and strength...and his charismatic appeal.

"Everybody liked him up there," recalled Duschen. "They just swarmed around him. We had a great turnout. We flew him up, put him up, and he more than paid his way."

"The Iowa State heavyweight was chiefly responsible for attracting an estimated 4,500 fans to the afternoon-evening session," wrote local sports editor Ed Kolpack. He added, "Taylor spent most of his time signing autographs when he wasn't on the mat."

Photo courtesy of Ames Tribune

He flattened his three foes in times of 35 seconds, 48 seconds and 86 seconds.

The Gentle Giant

In a second interview with Kolpack, Chris revealed the difficulty he was experiencing in adjusting to college life this time around.

"It was hard to get with it (studying) when I went back to school," he told Kolpack. "I couldn't get motivated. I was real close to being ineligible, but I'm okay now."

The Omaha Wrestling Tournament was the next stop, and ISU won all of the 30 matches it wrestled. The team finished with the maximum ten titles and 134 points. Chris won the award for the most falls, with three, and teammate Ron Glass was voted the most valuable wrestler. Just as in Fargo, the biggest story was Chris's power at the gate. He was largely responsible for luring 1,800 fans to the afternoon session and another 2,500 for the night finale.

Photo courtesy of Ames Tribune

"I went out there and shot a takedown...

He flattened his three foes in times of 35 seconds, 48 seconds and 86 seconds. He was provided a more intense workout by signing autographs for a long time at the conclusion of the meet.

The Midlands Tournament was aptly labelled a "mat monster" in 1972 by its organizers. The meet was at one time considered a "homey" two-day tournament for colleges in the Midwest. But by 1972, partly because of the mystique of Dan Gable, who claimed Midlands titles for six straight years, drawing hugh crowds, it had grown to a record 645 entries. Ten mats were hauled out for use in the opening session, with mats set up at two sites. The top four schools picked by *Amateur Wrestling News* were present: Iowa State,

Photo courtesy of Ames Tribune

In the dual meet season opener, Iowa State rolled over Nebraska 48-0 at Lincoln.

Michigan State, Washington and Oklahoma State. The advance ticket sales for 1972 were far ahead of the previous year. The LaGrange High School gym held 4,400 fans, and a complete sellout was expected for the finals.

Chris opened with a pin over Iowa's Jim Witzleb in 1:21, and Marquette's Ben Guido in 1:19. Rugged Michigan State star Larry Avery bowed 3-1, and Chris finished fast, pinning Michigan's Gary Ernst in 3:29 and Oklahoma State star Tom Hazell in 1:42.

"I went out there and shot a takedown; it was like hitting a brick wall," recounted the 245 pound Witzleb, a former junior national champion. "He grabbed me with one arm, lifted me up and tossed me down. I can remember thinking, 'What am I doing here?' "

Photo courtesy of Ames Tribune

Chris won by a pin over Jeff Class in 1:27.

Photo courtesy of Ames Tribune

Chris won by a pin, in 1:40 over Pete Clark...

It was a thought that became a common theme for the gentle giant's foes during the 1972-73 season. The huge star was developing his skills and maturing to a point where he was all but unbeatable.

In the dual meet season opener, Iowa State rolled over Nebraska 48-0 at Lincoln. Chris won by a pin over Jeff Class in 1:27. The next meet was the home opener at Ames, the first ever in new Hilton Coliseum. The season wrestling poster featured a photo of Chris holding Hilton off the ground, and quickly became a collector's item.

Chris's parents and sisters were among the thousands that came to the historic opener in Hilton. "This place sure could hold a lot of hay," remarked Jim when he entered the huge arena where his son would wrestle hours later.

The Cyclones broke in the facility with a 41-3 rout over Colorado State. Chris won by a pin, in 1:40 over Pete Clark, a three-sport star for the Rams who was drafted by the Dallas Cowboys of the NFL as a tight end.

On January 4, 1973, the Cyclones hosted Mankato State and dished out a 32-7 loss as Chris pinned Lee Theleman in 1:30. Four nights later, at Madison, Wisconsin, he took just 3:12 to pin Glenn Vissers in a 31-6 Cyclone victory. When ISU shut out Colorado 49-0 in a home appearance on January 12, he stopped Bark Enoch in 3:33.

On January 18, the Cyclones traveled to Iowa City for an historic interstate battle with the Iowa Hawkeyes. The two schools had not met on a wrestling mat since 1938, and the meet had a number of attractions. Not only was Iowa State rated No. 1 in the nation and bringing to town the nation's No. 1 wrestling attraction in Chris, but Cyclone legend Dan Gable was in the midst of his first year as the new assistant coach at Iowa.

The meet drew NCAA record crown of 10,268 fans. The Cyclones won seven of the ten matches for a 29-9 triumph, and received pins from freshman Pete Galea and Chris. The final pin of the night, over Iowa's Jim Waschek in 5:48, lifted Chris' season record to 21-0, with 19 pins.

Galea had become the squad's second leading pin artist, as a freshman. He first visited the ISU campus the year before as a New York high school senior, and had roomed with high school teammate Bob Antonacci. When Chris came into the room to welcome the two recruits, he picked up both Pete and Bob and set one on each of his shoulders, then put them down and left the room. The two high school stars were in awe of the gentle giant.

Both Antonacci and Galea declared for Iowa State, and entered as freshmen in the fall of Chris's senior season. One day shortly after arriving on campus, Galea was walking up a steep incline on Welch Avenue. Chris came up behind him on his 250 CC motorcycle, and shouted, "Hey, little buddy, hop on and I'll give you a ride."

Galea was flattered by the attention from the biggest star in town, and hopped on. But the incline was too much with both of them on the motorcycle.

"This isn't going to work," said Chris. He jumped off and pushed the motorcycle, with Galea on it, to the top of the hill.

It was a comic scene when Chris and his 300 pound friend, Ed "Huffy" Huffman rode through the streets of Ames on the motorcycle, with a combined weight of nearly 700 pounds. The two battled one another in the workout room day after day, week after week, and then took to the streets, and often the pizza houses to wind down. They were an unmistakable pair, wherever they roamed.

But Huffman wasn't Chris's only workout partner. He would also work out with the smaller wrestlers, partially from necessity (after all, there was a scarcity of men his size to practice with) and partially to work on his quickness. Often, he would lift them up over his head with one hand and put them down gently. It was exercise in playtime, like a dad with his little sons.

"I worked out with him about 30 or 40 times," admitted Gable, reflecting back to the days when the two superstars were in the Iowa State room together.

"I remember making a big mistake once. I let him start on top. I can't remember why, but if I let him start on top I was awful stupid back then.

"I tried a sit out, and he came down on me. It flattened me out - I was afraid to look down; I thought maybe a rib was sticking out, or poking in my heart. How much did I weigh? About 155. Chris was around 430 or 440."

But Gable also recalled a moment when he came out on top — if only for a second.

"One time, I caught him in a tiny move, a leg sweep. Honestly, when he hit the mat, the whole room shook. It was earth-shaking...it should have been, with 450 pounds flying through the air."

The team followed the Iowa victory with a three meet eastern swing. Chris pinned George Barkanich of Lehigh University in 1:50 as the Cyclones won 42-2. Then it was on to Franklin and Marshall University where Chris posted another pin in 1:34 and the team blanked the hosts 48-0. The third stop was at the Naval Academy, where a standing room only crowd of 4,000 saw Chris deck 205 pound Mark Salmen in 1:06 to cap the 35-5 Cyclone victory.

It was rumored a high ranking officer offered to give the Naval Academy heavyweight the Navy Cross for the valor he displayed in ever wrestling Chris.

The Cyclones returned home to host Hofstra University on January 24. Hofstra boasted a tough foe in heavyweight Joel Kislin, who was highly ranked nationally and had held Chris to a 5-2 decision the year before. The 310 pounder even went so far as to tell Anne Willemssen, a writer for the Iowa State student paper, that he was confident of a victory over Chris and it was "just a matter of mental preparation."

Chris was apparently taking the match seriously. Lynne said she could always tell when he was nervous before a big match by the number of peanut butter sandwiches he ate prior to the meet. And, he was wolfing them down before the Hofstra battle. The expected showdown failed to materialize, however, as Chris scored a pin in 3:59.

For all his fame on the wrestling mats, many who saw or read about Chris were fascinated by his eating patterns. They wanted to know how much he ate, how often, and what type of food. Stories about his eating were widespread throughout Ames and amateur wrestling circles, and Chris, always ready for fun, liked to add to the mythology of it all.

Returning from a road trip down South, Chris told Lynne of his experience in a restaurant in Chattanooga, Tennessee. The waitress, in a heavy Southern accent, asked Chris, Phil Parker and Carl Adams for their orders. She looked at Chris and said, "What can I get for you? "Chris simply responded, looking at his menu, "I want a half a side of beef and a garbage can full of lettuce, with a gallon of Thousand Island dressing." Startled, she began scribbling down the order until she realized he was kidding.

Often, Chris denied he ate much. However, most of those who had traveled with him felt differently.

"He always said he didn't eat any more than anyone else," said Gable, "and maybe he didn't at the table. But I noticed when I was with him that he was always snacking on something. He couldn't walk past a pop machine or a candy machine. He was always nibbling away at something, and that's where a lot of his weight came from, I would think."

Next, the top rated Cyclones traveled to Stillwater, Oklahoma, to meet the No. 2 ranked Oklahoma State Cowboys. It was a close call for the Cyclones, but they finally escaped from legendary Gallagher Hall with a 20-17 triumph. The Cyclones trailed 17-14 entering the final bout, but Chris scored a pin over rookie Dwight Cartwright in just 1:32 to lock up the win.

Al Nacin, the All-American 190 pounder, was usually Chris's roommate on the road. But on this particular trip to Oklahoma, Galea decided he would like to room with Chris.

Al was agreeable: "Okay, your tough luck kid," he told the unsuspecting freshman.

After the Oklahoma State meet, the two climbed into their beds. They talked for about 30 seconds, and Chris fell quickly into a sound sleep.

And then the snoring began. Finally at 4 a.m., Galea drug himself out of bed and staggered down the hall to Nacin's room. Galea decided there was no way he was going to try to roll Chris over onto his side to try to stop the snoring.

"Guys, let me in," pleaded Galea through the door to Nacin's room. "You've got to let me in. Chris is snoring so loud I can't get to

With 8,000 fans on hand, Chris extended his perfect record when he pinned 220 pound Dave Graves in 1:29

sleep."

Nacin mumbled an "I told you so, "and let Galea in, where he spent the remainder of the night on the floor.

Back home at Hilton, the Cyclones hosted the University of Washington on January 29, seeking revenge for their only setback the previous season. With 8,000 fans on hand, Chris extended his perfect record when he pinned 220 pound Dave Graves in 1:29. Graves had only lost once in his 11 previous matches, but made a critical mistake. He tried to shoot in low and get behind Chris, but the massive Cyclone sprawled on him, and then turned him for the quick pin.

After the match, Husky Coach Jim Smith offered his analysis of the Cyclone superstar.

"Taylor's not just big, he's plenty smart. He anticipated Grove's move. We're going to attack Taylor a little different next time. I still think Dave's got a chance to beat the big guy. He's not invincible — close, maybe — but not invincible."

Chris posted his fastest pin of the season when Iowa State faced Division II National Champion Cal Poly on January 31. He decked

Fred Stewart in a mere 43 seconds as the Cyclones won 31-9. On February 2, Iowa State shut out Southern Illinois when the Cyclones traveled to Carbondale, Illinois. Chris's pin came in 3:32 over Dan Robinson in the 41-0 romp. A second consecutive whitewash came the next night as the Cyclones hammered the University of Missouri, 42-0. Chris pinned Tom Cook in 3:15.

On the domestic front, life was progressing smoothly now that they were planning marriage. Lynne left her job at Younkers Department Store for a position at the 3M Company and moved into a new apartment, as well.

But life was somewhat more complicated for Chris than before the Olympics. He had become such a well-known celebrity that he could scarcely go anywhere without causing a number of stares.

"Before he became famous, girls always treated him sort of badly," said Huffman. "You know, he had warts around his neck, and he was conscious of them. He tried to cover them up. I think he had a lot of emotions inside that he bottled up. He always felt like the underdog, because of his size. But as his fame grew, he could have had lots of dates, if he had wanted to. But he and Lynne were real thick by then."

Amazingly, there were a few brave, and foolish, souls in Ames who were not afraid to antagonize Taylor. Several were even fool-hardy enough to push him into altercations.

The Cyclone star also received a number of requests for speeches, and fulfilled as many as he could work into his already tight schedule. He talked about his life, his wrestling career and answered questions. Many of the questions centered on the Olympics and his training. Chris always told the kids at the banquets to set goals for themselves.

Having been a Cub Scout back in his childhood days in Dowagiac, Chris eagerly accepted an opportunity to attend a Blue and Gold Banquet honoring scouts in Eagle Grove, Iowa. Chris and Lynne went with Bill Fjetland to attend the banquet as Fjetland was an Eagle Scout. Chris was the featured speaker at the banquet.

"He always enjoyed seeing people and signing the endless autographs," said Lynne.

"I know that some of these kids have gotten my autograph before, but I know it means a lot to them so I don't mind a bit," Chris said, when asked about signing autographs over and over again for the same kids.

Chris was chosen to represent Iowa State in the annual East-West All Star Wrestling Classic on February 5, 1973, at Lehigh

Chris eagerly accepted an opportunity to attend a Blue and Gold Banquet honoring scouts in Eagle Grove, Iowa.

"I know that some of these kids have gotten my autograph before, but I know it means a lot to them so I don't mind a bit," Chris said.

The Chris Taylor Story   77

University in Bethlehem, Pennsylvania. His opponent was Hofstra's Kislin, who was thirsting for revenge after being pinned earlier in Ames.

Shortly after the arrival of the two teams, a police car pulled up in front of Luke's Mid-City Restaurant in Bethlehem. After a moment the car began to rock back and forth, as though a struggle was going on in the back seat. It was not a matter for the law, however, it was just Chris trying to ease out the back door.

"I was walking over to the restaurant, when this police car stops me and wants to give me a ride after they recognized who I was," said Chris.

Chris won his match by injury default over Kislin. Chris led 2-0 early in the first period when all his weight came down on Kislin. For one instant, a total of 740 pounds (430 pounds of Taylor and 310 pounds of Kislin) was supported on Kislin's right knee, and it collapsed under the stress.

Chris stood over Kislin, staring down at the injured athlete, his face grimacing with concern. After a few moments, Kislin rose on one leg, with an arm across Chris's shoulders. Gently, Chris helped him hobble off the mat.

The match attracted the attention of Red Smith, the longtime sportswriter of the *New York Times*. For decades Smith had covered the biggest stories in sport, ranging back to the days of Jack Dempsey, Red Grange and Babe Ruth. He was considered far and wide the greatest sports writer in America, and to have him show an interest in amateur wrestling was an incredible coup.

"Chris Taylor rivals Disneyland as a tourists attraction, and the Iowa State team breaks attendance records wherever it goes," wrote Smith in his *New York Times* column.

"Taylor is a king size kewpie with red hair, blue eyes and a smile that is just plain sweet. He is an athlete, almost assuredly the best athlete of his size — or the biggest good athlete — in recorded history.

"Goliath stood 9 feet six inches, about three feet taller than Chris, but his won-lost record was 0-1."

Once again, Chris was categorized as a giant. And if Red Smith wrote it, it was nearly beyond dispute.

On February 9, the University of Oregon brought a team into Hilton, only to leave scoring a mere two points against the Cyclones. Iowa State handed the Ducks a 37-2 plucking and Chris laid Larry Ermini flat in 2:30. The following night, tough Oregon State showed up at the Hilton door, and the Beavers of Dr. Dale Thomas made a battle of it before bowing 20-11. Chris scored a 3-0 decision over Jim Hagen, a gusty 200 pounder who asked no quarter.

The following week a crowd of 8,000 witnessed the closest call Chris would experience as a Cyclone. Headlines all across Iowa screamed the unbelievable: "Taylor Almost Pinned." The Oklahoma Sooners came calling and a sophomore nearly got the best of him.

Bill Kalkbrenner, a rugged 235 pounder, scored a takedown and near fall in the opening seconds. As referee Keith Young of Cedar Falls lay on his stomach looking to see if the impossible had really happened, Chris managed to fight off his back. Trailing 5-0, he escaped and took the audacious Sooner down, scoring his own pin in two minutes and 29 seconds.

"It was close, the closest I've ever come to getting pinned since being at Iowa State," said Chris. "I really didn't expect it on my first move. I wound up in the wrong place, but I worked my way out of it."

The Big Eight Tournament was February 23 and 24 in Columbia, Missouri. Iowa State finished in second place with 94 points, behind champion Oklahoma State, and Chris took top honors in the heavyweight class for the second time. He pinned Nebraska's Jeff Class in 1:37, then won by disqualification over Missouri's Tom Cook and by default over Tom Hazel of Oklahoma State. He was on his way to the final stop of his collegiate career — the NCAA Tournament, on March 8-10 at Seattle.

Several of the Cyclones decided they needed to break the tension after the Big Eight meet. Twins Ron and Don Glass, Rich Binek and Pete Galea convinced Chris to go with them to a smorgasbord restaurant for an eating contest. Don and Pete were declared the winners; Chris opted to eat little, and enjoyed himself watching the others eat until they were miserable, chuckling loudly.

The Cyclones had one more appearance to make before the NCAA tourney started. They were at Drake University in Des Moines on February 27 and took the Bulldogs to the cleaners in a 46-0 romp. Chris pinned Don Bonner in 4:19.

All ten Iowa State wrestlers qualified for the three-day NCAA meet by virtue of their performances in the Big Eight, and ISU was heavily favored to win the team championship. Crowning two champions — Rich Binek at 177 and Chris, the Cyclones took home the title with 85 points. Oregon State came in second with 72.50, while Big Eight champion Oklahoma State tumbled to fifth, scoring just 42 points.

Chris made history by pinning all five of his foes. In all of NCAA history, only the legendary Danss Hodge of Oklahoma, in 1956 and

Gable of Iowa State in 1969, had pinned all their foes in an NCAA meet. His pins came in an aggregate time of 13:32 — less than three minutes per bout!

In the first round he put away Tony Policare from Buffalo in 2:26 and in the second round he pinned Joel Puelo of Duke in 3:28. Oklahoma State's Hazel went down in 2:39 in the quarterfinal, and Hofstra's Kislin was pinned in one minute flat in the semifinals. The final round saw Chris become a two-time NCAA champion as he pinned Jim Hagen from Oregon State in 4:19.

The awards ceremony at the NCAA tournament closed with a special presentation. Margaret Hays, a sculptor from Lynnwood, Washington, presented Chris with a marvelous bust she had made of him.

"I had returned to the University of Washington for a second degree," said Hays. "Although I had already had a degree in chemistry with a teaching certificate, I was pursuing a lifelong interest in sculpture. My husband's team had just won the city championships...I had spent a lot of time at wrestling meets and had read a great deal about Chris Taylor.

"The assignment in one of my sculpture classes was to do a bust. Because of my interest in wrestling I thought Chris Taylor

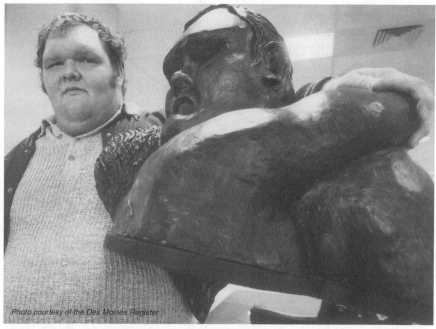

Margaret Hays, a sculptor from Lynnwood, Washington, presented Chris with a marvelous bust she had made of him.

Photos courtesy of the University of Washington

Chris Taylor, two time NCAA Champion, 1973, University of Washington.

Iowa State: NCAA champ

would be a marvelous subject. He had such striking look of sheer mass and power. I had never seen him in person, but had seen pictures of him, which I used as a source.

"The original was modeled in clay, then a plaster piece mold was made into which I laminated fiberglass and resin. I received an "A" on the project, put it away in my studio and went on to other projects.

"When I learned Chris Taylor was to be here (at the NCAA tournament in Seattle in 1973) it occurred to me that he might like to have it. By coincidence, the man who had done the announcing at the national tournaments, Ed Alverti, also was a faculty member at Lynnwood High School, where two of my children were attending, and a personal friend, as well. I asked him if he could get me access to the dressing room and Chris Taylor so I could give the bust to him.

"Chris won first that night and received his award last. Then two students carrying the sculpture escorted me to the front of the floor and I presented it to Chris in front of the whole crowd at the University of Washington. We only had a few words together. Chris was shy, modest. I never saw him again."

A note attached to the bust from Hays said, "Chris Taylor has captured the imagination of the country by the beauty of his size, skill and personality. My joy was in the creation; I hope he will find pleasure in possession."

The Gentle Giant

The bust sat in the seat next to Chris on the flight home from Seattle, and remains with his parents at the family farm in Dowagiac. They are very proud of it and relish showing it to visitors who have never seen it.

Shortly after the NCAA meet, Taylor pinned Henry Banke of Upper Iowa University in the Iowa All-Star Meet. With the final slap of the mat, the Chris Taylor era in collegiate wrestling came to a close. It had been short — just two years on the NCAA level, but extremely memorable. He compiled an 87-0-1 record for Iowa State, the tie with Oklahoma's Bill Sturve the only blemish, and captured two NCAA championships.

His 44 pins his senior year was an NCAA record. He was one of just three men to ever pin his way through an NCAA meet. Dan Hodge of the University of Oklahoma holds the highest percentage of pins over a three-year career, at .738, with Dan Gable (.730) and Rick Saunders (.723) close behind. Taylor's Iowa State percentage of .795 won't go into the record books because he didn't have a full three-year career, but his pin percentage speaks for itself.

Combining his records at Muskegon Junior College and Iowa State, Taylor fashioned a four-year mark of 143-5-1, with four of the setbacks coming in the Midlands. The question was being asked: "Is Chris Taylor the best heavyweight in collegiate history?"

The competition for such honorary distinction was fierce in 1973, even more so in 1988. Among the great heavyweight champions who preceded him were Earl McCready, who won three NCAA titles for Oklahoma State in the 1930s and never lost a college dual; Dick Hutton, a three-time NCAA champion for Oklahoma State in the 1940s, who was also runner-up in the NCAA's as a junior, narrowly missing becoming the only four-time champ in NCAA history; powerful Jim Nance, who lost just once in three years at Syracuse and was a two-time NCAA champion before moving on to the National Football League as a fullback, and Jess Lewis, the great Oregon State heavyweight who fashioned an 86-1 record, his only loss coming in the NCAA finals, 5-4, to Dave Porter, a senior who was winning his second championship.

Since Taylor's final year, the great heavyweights have continued. Jimmy Jackson was a 360 pounder who claimed three NCAA titles for Oklahoma State, and Lou Banach was a dynamic 210 pounder at Iowa who finished 1-3-1 in the NCAA's, and defeated behemoths like Tab Thacker (440 pounds) and Mitch Shelton (395 pounds).

"I may be a bit prejudiced, but I think Chris was the best heavyweight in college history," said Nichols years after Taylor's final bout as a Cyclone. "Anyway, I don't know of anyone who would have beaten him."

Duschen, the former Iowa State star who competed against many of the top heavyweights in the nation during and after college, thinks Taylor's prodigious size and strength would have been too much for any other heavyweight to contend with.

"I watched him mature at Iowa State," said Duschen, noted for his physical development and arm strength. "I was finished when he got there, but worked out with him a lot the first year."

"Chris seemed to hold back a lot in practice and in some matches, maybe because he was concerned about hurting someone. But when he went all out he was almost unstoppable.

"He was as strong as anyone I've ever seen. Once, he pressed 135 pounds overhead a couple of times with one hand. It was very hard to use strength against him, because he could stop yours, shut it down.

"There have been a few other massive heavyweights, a few guys who weighed around 400 pounds. But the thing that set Chris apart was he could really move on his feet. In the last two years or so, Medved was the only guy who could even really score on him."

Gable, who left Iowa State to guide the University of Iowa to nine straight NCAA team titles in the late 1970s and early 1980s agrees Taylor would have been very difficult to beat in college.

"He used his hips well, for movement and for good position, and that's one of the major keys to wrestling," said Gable. "He was also light on his feet, which was amazing, considering his weight. Also, most people were scared of him, and that was a big advantage.

"I don't think he was the best freestyle heavyweight we ever had. He really had a short career there, and Bruce Baumgartner (1984 Olympic champion and 1986 World Champion) would have been rated above him there. And I think some of the great heavy-weights, like Banach, would have given him a lot of trouble, even with the size difference. But the bottom line is, Chris was very tough to score on."

By the time his senior year arrived, Taylor was an athlete of awesome stature. The average time of pins during the 1973 season was 2:19 seconds — meaning that most opponents didn't even make it out of the first period. He had the experience of competing in the Olympics to help him mature, and it's hard to imagine any heavy-weight, of any era, being able to defeat the Gentle Giant who competed for Iowa State in 1973.

CHAPTER 9
Russ Houk's Mountain

"He never said, 'Will you marry me?" Lynne recalled years later. But for some time the two were talking about marriage. Finally, they set the date and the place: September 8, 1973, in Dowagiac. Chris surprised Lynne with a diamond and plans began to fall into place.

While Lynne was busy with wedding preparations, Chris embarked upon a new phase of his life, one that would eventually take precedence over almost everything else he hoped for. He began working summer wrestling camps. And it was heaven to him. He loved to work with kids, and the dream of someday owning and operating his own camps took root. One of the aspects he loved most was to see kids who wanted to go that extra mile, to put in that extra time in the off season, polishing their skills and techniques and practicing so that maybe someday they might be a champion, like the Gentle Giant who was teaching them.

The summer of 1973 was spent at Russ Houk's wrestling camp in the beautiful mountains of western Pennsylvania. Chris fell in love with it there, at the camp wrestlers referred to as "Russ Houk's Mountain". For a number of years, until Houk's ill health, it was home for the largest and most profitable non-campus wrestling camps in the United States. The mountain and the lake provide a breathtaking view, and after they were married, Lynne joined Chris there for up to six weeks each summer.

There is a knoll or hill on the camp site, the top of which overlooks a beautiful sixteen acre man-made lake. New arrivals always

The "L" shaped, Olympic size swimming pool.

Photo by Art Connorton

gather there, to take in the view of the lake to the front of the camp.

The "L" shaped, Olympic size swimming pool is a major attraction, and the coaches' house sits just down the hill. The bridge which leads to the playing fields is surrounded by the dense forest. There are other mountains beyond, but this particular one is Russ Houk's Mountain.

The serenity of the setting is broken only by the sounds of a wrestling camp in action. The electric chatter of the video games and the "tap-tap" of the ping pong balls coming from the screened recreation building or the clanging of barbell plates from the lifting area, next to the sauna and adjacent to the pool. The splashing and shouting of young athletes frolicking in the large pool, with its slides and diving boards, can be heard for half a mile.

Such is the excitement of the first day of wrestling camp every Sunday, when the new arrivals come. But one particular summer day, the coming of Chris Taylor will always be a special memory for all who were there.

High school heavyweights, huge young men, poured in from all over, anxious for the privilege of working out with 1972 Olympian Chris Taylor. Russ had broadcast the news far and wide that Taylor was working the camp that summer. By 3 p.m. most of the wrestlers had checked in.

Though they had not been instructed to do so, the young wrestlers gathered on the lawn outside the pool area. There were hundreds of them, anxiously awaiting Chris's arrival. At one point a huge man appeared at the top of the hill lumbering towards the pool.

"Is that him?" asked one of the wrestlers, staring at the horizon.

"That's him, I know it is," said another.

"Geez, I never thought he would really come," said yet another.

The chatter grew in volume as the giant paused on the crest of the hill. As they watched, a booming voice rang out from the other side of the hill.

"Hey, little man, how have you been?"

The giant on the hilltop turned toward the source of the voice. All eyes were fixed on top of the hill by now. A sun-bleached, red head rose above the crest of the hill as its owner climbed the other side of the hill. The shoulders came swaying into view, and then the mammoth chest in Olympic warm-ups came into view. The giant the kids had first seen was a "mere" 300 pound high school lad from California.

The booming voice sounded again: "Hey, California, you ready to wrestle?"

*Chris, Art &
Sherie Connorton
at Summer
Camp.*

Photo by Art Connorton

Rather than the customary cheering when heros arrive, silence
struck the wrestlers; words seemed insignificant. A "true" giant, at
least 150 pounds larger than the one who first appeared, was before
them.

The young wrestlers at the camp idolized Chris and breathed in
every word he said. And he returned their affection. He thoroughly
enjoyed being among them, recognizing the impact he could have on
their lives, their goals, their aspirations.

The truth lay submerged deep in the innermost part of Chris's
emotional makeup; perhaps author Sarah Teale had touched on it
most profoundly in her book, "Giants".

"Most giants tried to be accepted and liked by small men," she
wrote, speaking not only of the mythological giants that inhabit the
subconscious psyche of the human species, but also of the real-life
giants who so very infrequently show up in our midst. "Basically,
they were friendly by nature and loved companionship, but they
were easily hurt by rejection."

In a world that Chris found difficult to contend with from time
to time, facing the constant threat of rejection because of his out-
landish dimensions, he was almost always accepted in wrestling
circles. Wrestlers his own age stood in awe of him, after testing him
on the mat. And younger wrestlers looked upon him with an even
greater awe...a sense of wonder mixed with fear. Once his gentle
nature was proven to them, they couldn't resist the urge to be around
him, to stand next to him, to measure him, to try and catch his
eye...to be approved by a "giant", a truly unique human being.

To know a giant was a thrill most of them could only dream of
before meeting Chris Taylor. But, he made their dreams come true,

and they loved him for that.

Chris was one of the darlings of ABC Television during the 1972 Summer Olympics and kids everywhere who had seen the telecasts or had heard of him clamored to see him in person. They talked all day long about actually meeting him, shaking hands with him.

Art Connorton, a camp counselor, and his daughters were among those eager to see Chris. Art already knew Chris well, but his daughters had never met him. Yet, somehow the girls didn't happen to see Chris as he came into the cafeteria for supper, and did not even notice when he sat down at their table. He tapped Sherrie Connorton (the youngest of the Connorton girls, who was seven at the time) and said, "Wanna hot dog, kid?" She accepted the bun and started her first bite...then leaped up and backed away from the table. The hot dog had moved inside the bun. It was Chris's finger, with mustard spread on it. Everyone at the table roared and a friend-ship between Chris and the Connorton girls, Cindy, Sherrie and Tracy, was under way.

The girls attended every session Chris taught that week and he rewarded them after each one by roughhousing with them and letting them sit on his shoulders and extended arms. He gave them all "Chrissy-back-rides" across the bridge.

The third year Chris worked Russ's camp, he was going through his passing out the mail routine with the boys. He took the last envelope, which belonged to the camp "wise guy" and opened the letter, smelled the stationery and exclaimed, "Hmmm...this could be a love letter."

Chris and other camp counselors at Russ Houk's Mountain wrestling camp.

The Gentle Giant

He began to read: "Dear Billy, I love you so much and can't wait until you get home Friday night and we can go in your car down to the river." Chris continued for a few minutes in the same vein, and then wrapped it up: "Billy," he said, staring at the young wrestler, "you act bad, but if someone loves you this much you must be a nice guy on the inside."

As Billy walked away totally embarrassed, Chris added a message to the 300 boys who were watching and listening to every word.

Chris working with young wrestlers - June 1973.

"I was fooling about the letter, it's from Billy's dad; but he is a good guy."

Properly, and gently chastised for his unbecoming manners, Billy was put in his place. He caused no more trouble at camp. He eventually became a wrestling coach working with young boys who aspire to greatness.

At another session, Chris finished up one of his talks and asked for questions. A little, towheaded 10-year-old raised his hand gingerly. Chris walked over to him and asked, "What's the trouble little man?"

The boy looked up, eyes wide and asked, "Chris, are there any bears in these woods?"

Chris perceived the older wrestlers had been teasing the little guy. He stood over the seated boy, crossed his big arms over his huge chest and turned his gaze to the horizon, first to his left and then to his right. Using his booming voice to full dramatic effect, he said, "Son, do you see any bears?"

"No," the little boy answered.

Chris's voice boomed again: "That's because they know Chris is here."

The entire camp cheered as the little towhead took a deep breath and sighed his relief. The remainder of the week, everywhere Chris went on the camp grounds that lad was beside him, walking quickly along and often reaching up to hold Chris's pinkie finger.

The trampoline was off limits on Houk's Mountain unless spotters were present on all four sides, for safety reasons. Quite a crowd gathered one bright summer day when Chris announced he would be on the trampoline in ten minutes. Knowing Chris and his antics, one could assume that being "on" the tramp perhaps meant he would be on the tramp sunbathing, or reading or anything else.

The campers streamed to the site, speculating on how the trampoline would probably touch the ground, or snap in the incredible impact of 450 pounds landing on it over and over. All the buzzing stopped when Chris arrived. He hopped up on the trampoline backwards, and then rolled to the middle of the trampoline. It was obvious that he had been there before.

He began to bounce, and was so light on his feet that the trampoline did not seem taxed at all. He did a few seat drops, knee drops and belly drops and the kids went wild. They had not been prepared for how agile he was, and the shock of seeing him cavort on the trampoline was exhilarating to them all.

Chris then announced he was going to attempt the highest flip in the history of man. Who could doubt him? He bounced six or seven times, flying higher with each effort, and his size viewed from the angle of the four foot high trampoline made it seem to a young boy like he was going to hit the clouds. He stopped bouncing suddenly and asked, "Are you ready?"

A chorus of kids shouted, "Yes!"

Chris bounced again and yelled out, "Here goes!"

He then flipped right at mat level, stood abruptly and raised his arms, dismounted and walked away as the kids cheered wildly. The "highest flip" was only about six inches above the mat! Chris had proven himself a master showman.

Later, the coaches' wives were pleased about finding a good buy on 16 ounce bottles of soft drinks, and purchased two cases. That evening in the living room of the coaches' house, Chris walked in with a bottle of cola. One of the wives asked, "Did you find the deal on the 16 ounce bottles too, Chris?"

Chris smiled and held out his bottle, and said, "This is a quart, little lady." In his massive hand, the bottle had appeared far smaller than it actually was.

After a teaching session the coaches would often work out in the middle of the pavilion. Chris was the catalyst who always got everyone involved, a real thrill for the coaches who were at the camp as students this week.

Chris often wore a huge gold football jersey, with no numbers on it. One particular day, Art was experiencing one of those low energy days that hits after about ten consecutive weeks at camp, and was staying removed from the action.

"You getting old, Art?" Chris teased.

Art waved him off. He was sitting on the mat and Chris walked up behind him, gripped him under one arm pit, lifted him to a standing position and pulled his jersey over Art's head, down to his waist. The two were inside the gold tent. Art couldn't see. He wrapped his arms around Chris in a bear hug that just about reached.

Art scrunched Chris and waited to hear the familiar expulsion of breath that always followed when someone used a bear hug on a foe. But there was no sign Chris was even slightly affected. Was Chris Taylor so tough he wouldn't give even a little to Art's hug? He scrunched Chris again. Nothing! Suddenly, it was light again. Chris had lifted the shirt and he bellowed, "What are you doing there, little man?"

Art's bear hug was tight all right...high on Chris's thigh.

Chris possessed unbelievable strength. Through all his experiences with the Olympics and wrestling, Houk never met anyone with the strength to match Chris. It was an opinion shared by thousands of others.

His Iowa State teammates once talked Chris into joining in a power lifting competition. Like many naturally strong men — Dan Hodge and Tom Peckham, for example — he had never done much weight training, but the Iowa State crew convinced him to tag along with them to the meet. Once in the gym, he was talked into competing. He walked over, dead lifted the bar, the weights clanging loudly on the ends, straight up from the floor to a standing position — and won the competition. He had beaten everyone; or as one friend said, "He put everyone to bed."

Huffman recalled the time when a large fellow with bulging muscles was showing off at a party. He finished up by lifting the front of a Volkswagon car off the ground, a good feat but not overly impressive as the engine is in the rear. Without hesitating, Chris walked to the back of the Volkswagon and lifted the rear off the ground.

"He pulled it about four or five feet off the ground, and just held it there," said Huffman, chuckling at the recollection. "That other guy had been trying all night to show off."

When Lynne and Chris moved into the Hillcrest apartment complex in Dowagiac shortly after their marriage, Tom Lawrence helped them. The apartment was on the second floor of the complex and everything had been moved in, with the exception of the king-size mattress.

"I was dreading it, but the mattress had to go up somehow," said

Lawrence.

"Let's get this thing moved in, TL," said Chris. "Get up on the balcony."

Lawrence questioned his friend's logic, but Chris was so insistent that Lawrence went to the balcony. Chris walked back to the truck, grabbed the mattress, folded it like a piece of bread, and tossed it up onto the balcony, as though it only weighed a couple of pounds. The problem of moving that mattress was solved.

Chris never liked heights. As a young child Jim and Vera had a tough tim keeping him off ladders, but years later he had no time for ladders or high places. Once, Lawrence and some friends were roofing a house and Chris came by to help. They all knew Chris didn't like heights.

"What do you think you can help with?" asked Lawrence.

"I don't know, but there must be some way I can help," replied Chris. The rest of the crew was on top of the roof putting new shingles in place. They had all climbed down when Chris arrived.

"I know what I can do," said Chris. "You guys get back up there."

The others climbed up on the roof. Then, Chris picked up the 90 pound bundles, one at a time, and handed them to the men on the roof, with one hand.

There were occasions, however, when his weight was a hindrance rather than a benefit.

"He always tried to get the strongest chair in a place, wherever we went," recalled Huffman. "Once he sat down in this chair and it just blew. It sounded like it disintegrated. He had slivers in his rear," said Huffman with a chuckle.

Photo by Art Connorton

The bridge over the creek formed by the run-off drain.

At Russ's Mountain, the barbells and plates were stored on A-frame iron racks outdoors. When it rained, they had to be carted inside to avoid rust damage. One day a sudden storm broke out and the staff ran to the A-frame rack, ready to start removing all the plates and take them inside.

"What is going on here, little men?" Chris asked.

They explained. He stepped next to the A-frame rack, lifted the rack complete with plates, and carried it up a small knoll, to the building. There, he stopped and faced the group and performed his famous "bip-bip" muscle movement routine, flexing his biceps, first one then the other with each "bip".

For years the bridge over the creek formed by the runoff drain from the man-made lake at Russ's Mountain had been sufficient, but with the increased camp enrollment the bridge needed to be replaced. Chris convinced Russ it should be replaced immediately and the project would be a great activity for the coaches to do themselves.

A truck crane came up the mountain, lifted the arched "I" beams for the bridge into place, and then departed. When the wrestling session ended, Chris called his work crew together for some "fun". The wood cross supports had been precut. It was discovered the "I" beams were perfect on one end of the bridge, but six inches off at the

Photo by Art Connorton

Chris, John Peterson and Sherie Connorton at Summer Camp.

other end. It looked like the crane would have to be called back for additional work.

The support on the good end was bolted in place, and John and Ben Peterson and Russ Hellickson, all three Olympic medalists and extremely powerful men, tried to set the odd end in place. Randy Watts and Art Connorton held the other end up and Chris,

Chris receiving the 1973, Big Eight Conference Athlete of the Year Award.

the human crane, climbed down among the rocks, stood under the "I" beam, and pressed it over his head. He took a tiny step forward and lowered it down for perfect placement.

"The next day was spent putting support poles on the footings, each of which Chris held upright while the other coaches bolted the telephone poles in place," said Connorton.

"The floor boards of the bridge were to be nailed in place with a one-half inch gap to allow for expansion and contraction due to seasonal changes. As the crew of six worked and goofed around, the gap kept narrowing as the installation progressed. It was then suggested that we pull out about 20 feet and do it correctly.

"Taking the boards out was harder than installing them! The spikes had gone through the support beams. After much toil, it was discovered that it was easy if they hammered the nails up from the bottom and had 'the crane' pull the boards up with his bare hands. I tried one, but it wouldn't move at all. Chris 'one handed' it and then did his "bip-bip" routine as the group howled with laughter.

The bridge was complete in two days.

As his fame spread, he was invited to appear in the Strong Men's Competition sponsored by CBS Television. After the wheelbarrow event, Chris had a gigantic lead. He went last, and won by nearly 10 seconds. He also knocked several seconds off the existing record.

The next event was weight lifting. He arrived at the site late due to being the last competitor in the wheelbarrow event. The shadows from the sun had moved due to the delay and the platform had to be moved, as well. the loaders began removing the plates from the bar, still loaded from the last contestant. Chris picked up the bar, held it for a few seconds while the platform was relocated, and then set it down in the center of the platform.

Near summer's end in 1973, Chris was asked to attend a gathering in Kansas City at the Big Eight Conference headquarters. He had been named the conference's Athlete of the Year, an award that usually went to football or basketball players. He flew to Kansas City, attended the ceremony, and took his trophy back with him to Russ's Mountain to share with his friends.

Meanwhile, Lynne was in Dowagiac taking care of last minute wedding preparations. The time was closing in on the wedding date before it dawned on them that they had neglected to pick up their marriage license. Fortunately, Chris knew someone at the county government offices and made arrangements to get it picked up. With the detail out of the way all systems were go for the wedding.

Invitations had been mailed out to friends all over the United States. Gifts began to arrive at the Taylor home. The wedding party included Lynne's twin sister, Lsybeth, as maid of honor, and Dean Claborn as best man. Lynne's sister Leatrice, and Chris's sisters, Sherrie and Becky, stood up with her, while Ed Huffman, Chuck Burling and Jimmie Klees were groomsmen.

The wedding rehearsal was held at the First Christian Church in Dowagiac. The minister was new and relatively inexperienced, having performed only three weddings previously. Lynne and Chris kidded him by saying they had decided to just shake hands at the end of the ceremony instead of the traditional kiss.

The rehearsal dinner was held at the Taylor farm, in beautiful weather. Pheasants were roasted over a big fire. The party continued until 4 a.m. as the rehearsal dinner turned into a bachelor party.

"I was concerned Chris would not be at the church on time," said Lynne. "We were at the church by noon, the wedding was set to begin at 2 p.m. Chris was a bit late, but only because he had gone to the care home first to visit with his great grandmother, who was in her 90s at the time. Chris wanted to make sure she got to the church and went to get her himself."

Lynne's brother, Robert Hart, Jr. gave the bride away as her father was deceased. Her mother, Frances, was seated in the front row, and saw her daughter come down the aisle in the traditional long white gown with a white veil. Her attendants wore yellow and white, and red and white gowns with matching veils. Chris and his attendants wore blue suits with yellow shirts. Chris had a blue suit especially made for the occasion at Gilberts in South Bend, Indiana.

A full house of 500 people, some of whom spilled over outside, attended the wedding. Chris sweated profusely during the nuptials and the minister's hands shook so bad that Chris and Lynne giggled to each other during the ceremony.

They left the church and headed out to Twin Lakes Road to the Taylor farm for the reception. Canopies were set up on the lawn to accommodate the 500 guests. Friends prepared two hogs, and twelve turkeys, with all the trimmings. The reception continued until well after 10 p.m.

The newlyweds spent their wedding night in South Bend. The next day they visited Ames before starting their trip out west. They wanted to visit Chris's uncle, Bob Taylor, in Boise, Idaho, and see the many sights along the way. Boise was also the home of Mike Young, a longtime friend of Chris's and the head wrestling coach at Boise State College. Young invited Chris to work out and talk to his wrestlers during practice.

Incredibly, Chris worked out with a man who actually out-

Chris and Dean Clayborn at Chris and Lynne's wedding.

Other Taylor friends with Chris and Jim Taylor at the wedding reception.

The Gentle Giant

weighed him — for the first and only time in his entire life. Chris weighed 430 pounds during the visit, and Mark Bittick, the Boise heavyweight, weighed in at 460 pounds. Local photographers had a field day snapping photos of the two, while the other wrestlers shook their heads in amazement.

The couple left Boise for Las Vegas, where they spent time playing slot machines. They then headed to Oklahoma City to see Wayne Wells, the 1972 Olympic champion at 163 pounds and a teammate of Chris's in Munich. Wells earned his law degree while working to make the Olympic team, and was representing Chris in some legal matters. They discussed Chris's future plans, and what avenues he should pursue. He was two quarters shy of graduating from Iowa State and despite urging from Lynne, Chris's parents and friends to get his degree, he was leaning towards a career in professional wrestling. Chris knew if he turned professional, it would kill his amateur status and thus eliminate him from any future Olympic competition.

The national spotlight shined brightly on Chris during his brief time at Iowa State. He was featured in many newspapers, national magazines and television shows, by some of the greats in those fields. The likes of Heywood Brown of CBS, Merle Harmon of TVS Sports, Red Smith of the *New York Times*, and Herman Weiskopf of *Sports Illustrated* had all focused on him. The NCAA filmed features of Chris, and he was discussed on popular television shows like Rowan and Martin's "Laugh-In" after his Olympic appearance.

And always, Chris found time for his fans, and especially

Photo by Art Connorton

Chris, Lynne and Chris's uncle and aunt in Boise.

children. The Sports Information Department at Iowa State even received notes from opposing schools, thanking Chris for taking time after meets to sign autographs and have pictures taken. He was indeed loved by the nation, the state of Iowa and by the fans...and he returned the affection.

He had become a national celebrity, and professional wrestling seemed to him a natural step for a man who had always enjoyed playing to the crowd and being the center of attention. Faced with the end of his scholarship aide and with the new demands of married life, he was ready to put amateur wrestling behind him and to use his size and skill to earn pay for his efforts. Even if it meant passing up the 1976 Olympics in Montreal.

"I've no regrets at all about missing the 1976 Olympics," Chris told a reporter. "I've taken a few knocks here and there and I'm glad I'm done. There are certain goals I set in life. One of them was to go to the Olympics, but not necessarily to win a medal. I won a medal and I was really happy about that. I feel like I've been there — been where I wanted to go and now it's time to settle down and raise a family and make my wife happy, if nothing else."

There may have been another factor in his decision to turn professional. Not only was he tired of being without money, but he knew that to improve upon his 1972 Olympic performance, he simply had to beat the Soviets. After Medved retired in 1972, it was assumed by many fans around the world that the American giant was the heir apparent to the throne.

But in 1973, the Soviets came up with up another heavyweight of tremendous ability. Chris and Soslam Amdiyev tangled in June in 1973 in Madison Square Garden in New York. The rangy, six-foot seven inch Soviet took Chris down four times, and scored a 4-1 victory. The Soviet team also won 5-4-1. A win by Chris would have given the United States its first victory ever in a dual meet with the Soviets.

For whatever reason, Chris seemed incapable of beating the Soviets. He had a lifetime record of 0-7 against them. That fact could have played a role in Chris's decision to try his hand at professional wrestling.

At any rate, Chris decided to become a professional athlete after returning from his honeymoon. In December of 1973 he began a kind of wrestling unlike anything he had ever done before.

CHAPTER 10
After the Wedding

Lynne and Chris moved to Minneapolis during Chris's training period in his new found profession of professional wrestling. They found an attractive apartment near several of Minnesota's famous 10,000 lakes, and settled in. But Chris came home from the workouts sore and exhausted.

"He was very physically tired, he thought he was going to die," Lynne recalled. "He was so sore. He would come home and fall asleep. He even needed help getting dressed, he was so sore from professional wrestling."

Chris the professional wrestler.

After passing muster, Chris went on the road, wrestling primarily in the upper Midwest and the West Coast. He entered the ring in his long Iowa State robe, wearing an Olympic style singlet. Lynne traveled with him for much of the first year, and they tore from town to town, day after day. It was a maze of times and dates, days blurring into weeks.

A normal week would include a Saturday night show in Chicago, a Sunday night show in Green Bay and a drive back to Minneapolis, ending at 4 a.m., a Wednesday night and Thursday night match, and then flights to North Dakota and Canada for matches on Friday and Saturday nights.

Another schedule included ten days of matches and travel in Texas, followed by a drive to North Dakota. On a number of occasions. Lynne flew to Dallas to pick Chris up at the airport. There were other times when she drove to Chicago to see him in the midst of a ten-day tour.

The popularity Chris enjoyed as an amateur was mostly evidenced in professional wrestling's youngest fans. The kids idolized him, and yearned to be around him.

When Dean Claborn went to watch Chris wrestle in Detroit he

was told to meet Chris fifteen minutes after his match was complete so they could leave the building right away. As they were leaving they heard someone say, "There's Chris Taylor." The two turned and saw kids running down the hall at them.

"Chris stopped and waited for them to catch up," said Claborn. "He shook their hands and answered their questions. They hung on him and felt his muscles. He just stood there and shook his head. He knew he had to stop, and as much as he wanted to leave, it wasn't his nature to do so."

Through the trials and tribulations, he remained the same gentle giant, exhibiting the same personal magnetism that had made him so popular in college and in summer camps. He still found time to sign autographs and talk to the kids.

Chris started out as a star; the *People Magazine* article of March 11, 1974, noted he had compiled a perfect 30-0 record in his months on the tour. But despite his early success, pro wrestling caused a great deal of concern among Chris's family and friends. Jim and Vera weren't in favor of it, but at the same time they knew it was something Chris felt he had to do. At first he didn't feel that wrestling professionally was a very prestigious career, but it had been his decision and he thought he could make some fast money and get out.

His family and friends respected his decision, but were worried he would not really benefit from the career he had selected. Once when Vera expressed an interest in going to one of his matches, Chris simply said, "Mom, you don't want to see that." She never did.

At the same time, Chris defended the game to those who had the temerity to question it. Often, he would merely shrug his shoulders and offer a halfhearted explanation. But at other times, he would be more emphatic.

"It's hard work. It's a lot harder than people think. I didn't use to think it was real either...but it is," he told a reporter during his first year on the job.

"If professional wrestling is fake, I wish somebody would tell me about it. I've had an ankle swollen twice the regular size it should be and I've lost a couple of teeth. It's like skiing, I guess you could say. Watching it doesn't really look that hard, but when you try it, it is."

"I remember one time at a summer camp when a certain coach was giving Chris a bad time about professional wrestling as being fake," said Pete Galea. "It started to get under Chris's skin so he put him in a sleeper hold and as the guy was passing out, Chris said, 'Was that fake?' "

Tom Blecker, a former high school wrestler who knew Chris and the Iowa State team of that era well, also experienced the infamous sleeper hold once.

"I was teasing Chris about professional wrestling being fake," recalled Blecker. "I told him the sleeper hold was really phony. Well, Chris grabbed me and put it on me right there. I could feel myself passing out. I was going to drop to the floor, but he stopped and let

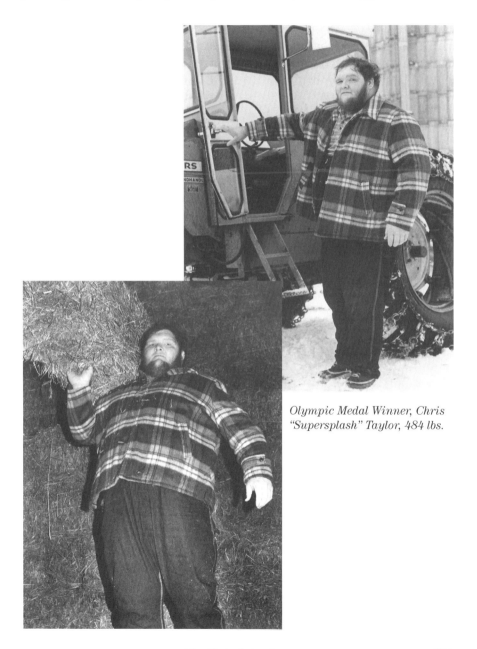

Olympic Medal Winner, Chris "Supersplash" Taylor, 484 lbs.

me go. He was so strong I couldn't believe it. And the sleeper really works, I can tell you that!"

For some reason Chris never seemed to click in pro wrestling. Much of the problem could undoubtedly be attributed to his emotional makeup. Pro wrestling by most accounts, is a game for solitary-type personalities, men content to be alone for long periods of time.

The long drives between matches, the hectic schedule, the roughhousing, and his excessive weight all began to exert their toll on Chris. The drain on the huge body, which had gone over the 500 pound mark, was immense.

CHAPTER 11
A Daughter is Born

"Most giants were...seen as possessing great strength and sturdiness, although our researches clearly indicated that they were quite frequently plagued with physical ailments which rendered their lives wearisome and painful," wrote author Sarah Teague in her book, Giants.

"Paradoxically, many giants were whimsical and friendly rather than aggressive, and they often suffered curious inferiority complex problems due to their lumbering size."

She was writing about giants in general, but might have been writing specifically about Chris Taylor. He did possess great strength and sturdiness...but he was frequently plagued with physical ailments. At times, those elements surely rendered his life wearisome and painful.

As a college athlete, he admitted in an interview with *Sports Illustrated* he sometimes wished he was normal sized, and didn't always have to prove himself. And by his second year of professional wrestling, the physical ailments were catching up to him in a frightening manner.

In the summer of 1975, he was traveling continually. Lynne took a trip to Michigan to visit family and friends. While she was there she received an urgent phone call from a hospital in Davenport, Iowa. Chris had collapsed in the locker room prior to a bout, suffering from a deep blood clot in his leg. He had been experiencing ongoing problems, diagnosed as phlebitis at one point, with his legs and had actually blacked out briefly earlier in the day. He was taken to the hospital by ambulance and was in intensive care.

"He got a sore in his leg and didn't take care of it," said Lynne. "It apparently became infected."

Chris was eventually transferred to a hospital in Kalamazoo, Michigan; all together, he was hospitalized for nearly a month. When he was released, he still needed time to recuperate, but some viewed his recovery as more proof of his larger-than-life persona.

"Chris seemed indestructible, even in a confrontation with death," wrote one reporter. "Chris looked death in the eye and lived to tell about it. Chris, up against his most relentless foe, won again. When Chris wrestles again it should be a breeze, considering that he has won the most important bout of his career — the night death came to grapple and fled empty handed."

It was, unfortunately, just the first round in the skirmish with death. The fact was, Chris had begun a long, downhill slide health-wise. He would never fully recover.

He finally returned to the pro circuit, and traveled to Oregon. But his heart was no longer in it. He began thinking more and more about the great summer camps he had been a part of at Russ's Mountain. He

Chris with his daughter Jennifer, at the Taylor home in Dowagiac, MI.

began laying plans for a wrestling camp of his own. Yet, he was in no position financially to start a camp. The illness had placed a large drain on their money resources, taking away his ability to earn a living for a long period of time.

On October 7, 1975, Lynne gave birth to their daughter, Jennifer, at 2:25 p.m. She was born in Lee Memorial Hospital in Dowagiac, the same hospital that brought her father into the world. She weighed in at eight pounds and eight ounces, more than Chris had weighed twenty-five years earlier. The event made front page in the Dowagiac newspaper, which reported, "Taylor and his wife, Lynne, are currently residing with his parents (while Chris was) recuperating from an injury he sustained several months ago while wrestling professionally."

Amidst the pain he was feeling, Jennifer's birth was a source of great joy to Chris. Longtime friend Chuck Burling said Chris "was more high about her birth than I ever saw him before. He worshiped the ground that baby crawled on."

After the euphoria of being a father wore off, Chris returned to the reality of pro wrestling. He left for Oklahoma, where he worked out of Tulsa for Leroy McGuirk's Championship Wrestling organization. While there, he traveled for a spell with Dan Hodge, one of the true legends of wrestling, amateur and professional. "Chris rode to some matches with me. He was quiet, sort of a loner at this point, but then so was I when I was his age," said Hodge.

The two former amateur legends hit it off well. Hodge was always the star attraction at the matches, but Chris wrestled in the special main event leading into Hodge's match.

"I only knew him for a couple of weeks," said Hodge. "We mostly talked about amateur wrestling. He's asked me questions about my days in Oklahoma, and we'd talk about all sorts of wrestling stories."

"Some of the other wrestlers sort of shunned him, and said nasty things about his warts. But I took him under my wing. There were a lot of "ooooohhhss' and 'aaaaahhhsss', when he would use one of his Olympic throws. It's hard to go into another wrestler's backyard, without being real well known. But I think he would have been a big hit, if he hadn't gotten ill."

Lynne, Jennifer, and Chris, prior to his death. Photo taken at a restaurant in Story City, Iowa.

The leg problems flared again, and Chris wound up in University of Iowa Hospitals in Iowa City. He later told a friend he felt humiliated the way he was treated in Iowa City. He was growing despondent over his health.

"I've been injured more since I turned professional than ever in my life," he said in an interview at the time.

"There are no slouches in this business. You just don't catch a guy that isn't any good."

"I almost died from blood poisoning at one time recently when an abscess formed in my leg and all of a sudden it broke and spread throughout my body. I had a temperature of 105 and spent three and a half months in and out of the hospital."

But even though he was desperately ill at times, he maintained a brave front for friends who came to visit.

"I would usually find out he was in the hospital after he was already gone," said Gable, who was coaching less than a mile away from University of Iowa Hospitals. "But one time I got there and he was still there. He was real jovial and tried to hide how he felt. I left thinking he probably wasn't in too bad of shape."

Once while hospitalized in Iowa City, Chris received a number of handmade cards from the second grade class at Robert Lucas School. The class had heard he was in the hospital and wanted to let him know that they cared about him. It touched him deeply, and when he was released he visited the class before leaving town.

In January of 1979, Lynne and Chris decided to move back to Iowa for good. They found housing too expensive in Ames, but found a duplex they liked in Story City, located ten miles north of Ames. They felt the location was ideal — close to Ames and their friends there, and not too far from Minneapolis, if Chris decided to continue wrestling.

But Chris's wrestling days were over. He was plagued by more health problems, and was in and out of hospitals for tests and treatments. He was suffering from chronic hepatitis and liver problems. More telling, his weight, which he always carried with a certain majesty, started to sag.

For the down payment on the duplex, Chris went to his former wrestling coach, Dr. Nichols, and requested a loan. Nichols gave it to him without hesitating. Lynne returned to work at the 3M Company where she had been employed several years earlier, and Chris, unemployed, began baby-sitting Jennifer. He continually wrote on sheets of paper, outlining his plans for the future.

"As a wrestler it looks like I'm all through," he told a reporter. "I don't miss the constant traveling, but I will miss the sport. I'm a little itchy, but I realize it's going to take time to whip my illness. The people of Iowa have always been good to me.

"I want to stay here in Iowa, we just bought our new home here. I have about thirty tablets of paper written full of ideas. Maybe an answer is in one of those sheets."

Even in his last days, Chris maintained a loyalty to his friends that was amazing, and heartwarming. Art Conorton of Rochester, New York, invited him to be the featured speaker at the banquet honoring his team's high school wrestling season, and Chris had accepted months earlier.

Connorton picked Chris up at the airport, and could see immediately he was not well. His huge friend seemed to have filled up with water, and had lost much of his muscle tone. At a press conference in Connorton's home, Chris answered all of the same questions he had been asked for years about his size, appetite and the like. He did so with patience and understanding, said Connorton.

"Chris spoke at the banquet and everyone in the place could tell he was not well," said Connorton years later. "He let them know by example that it didn't matter; the real issue was the audience themselves and what they could do with their lives."

Chris told them that night, "To achieve, you must set goals and make a commitment to attain those goals. No goals should be too high. Get an education, become a champion, an Olympian, a medalist. It can all be attained by those of you who commit and try."

He closed to a long, emotional standing ovation. On the way

back to Connorton's, he kidded about an Iowa State wrestler being applauded for public speaking. He was in good spirits, despite his condition.

At the house, Chris shocked the Connortons, including the daughters who had fallen for him in the summer camp years ago. He told them he had to sign back in the hospital in Iowa the next day.

"What do you mean, sign in?" Connorton asked, shocked.

Chris revealed he had signed himself out of the hospital, relieving the hospital of any responsibility for his welfare, all in order to speak to a group of high school athletes and their parents, two thousand miles away.

"Chris, that was crazy!" exclaimed Connorton, shaken and concerned for his friend's well being. "You didn't have to do that."

Chris grinned: "Little man, I couldn't let those kids down. I promised them I'd be here."

Back in Iowa, Chris continued to plan summer camps. He was still a celebrity, and in demand at various public functions. He served as the honorary referee at amateur boxing matches after the speech in New York, and the following week he drove to Ellsworth Junior College in Iowa Falls, where he was the star attraction at yet another wrestling camp.

Though most of his close friends were very concerned with his deteriorating health, obvious by his continually sagging physique and loss of weight, nearly all were shocked at the sudden ending. In the early evening of June 30, 1979, Chris died in his sleep at home in Story City. The efforts of a local rescue team failed to revive him on the way to the hospital. He had died the day after the camp ended.

"I knew his time was short," recalled Huffman years later from his home in Florida. "He had told me a couple of weeks earlier that his dad wanted him to come back to Michigan. He was going to give Chris a few acres, and help him build a house.

"Chris said he owed everything to his dad, that he and his mom taught him manners, and to respect others. Chris would never walk away from anyone.

"But Chris didn't want to leave the Ames area. He had so many friends there. Heck, he was living in the past, but then we all do.

"He said he didn't have any money. I know he never made much from pro wrestling, not anything like people thought he did. But he never bad-mouthed pro wrestling. It was his profession.

"The last week he lived he was at a wrestling camp in Iowa Falls. He told Bill Delaney, the Ellsworth coach, that he really wanted to get a camp going, and Bill said, 'Hey, let's do it!' For a whole month, Chris was caught up in that camp. He was the happiest I'd ever seen him. We used to sit up half the night and talk when he got back."

The camp ended on Friday, June 29. He and Huffman had plans to get together that following night.

Huffman and his wife, Diane, were on their way to meet Chris the evening of June 30, driving from their home in Alden to Story City. But they got in an argument, and turned around and returned home. Minutes later, the phone rang.

"It was Mom," said Huffman. "She said it was on the news that Chris had died. I didn't believe it! Then Lynne called, and told us. It was unbelievable."

Huffman and other friends, some who lived in the Colonial Inn in Ames at the same time Chris did, banded together. They stayed up all night and rehashed fond memories they had spent with their gentle giant.

"I don't know how much worse I could have felt," said Huffman. "For ten years we were inseparable, we considered ourselves family. It was the worst thing that ever happened to me at that point.

"I do know Chris had some of the happiest moments of his life that last week."

Lynne was unsuccessful in her first attempt to reach Jim and Vera by phone; they were in South Bend shopping for Chris's birthday present. When she finally got through, Jim needed to find Sherrie and Becky, who were on a camping trip. Jim called Dean Claborn, and the two left late at night to the camp area near Baldwin, Michigan. With the help of local police, they located Chris's sisters around 1 a.m.

A memorial service was held July 31 in Ames, under the direction of Harry Burrell, former Sports Information Director at Iowa State. The funeral was held two days later at the United Methodist Church in Dowagiac. Rev. Tim Mertah, who had married Chris and Lynne less than six years earlier, performed the ceremony. Claborn, Huffman, Chuck Burling, Tom Lawrence, Craig Behnke, Mike Clark, Mike Leitz, Danny Robinson, Allan Smith, Pat Murphy, Carl Clark, Bill Heriman and John Lewis were pallbearers.

Chris was buried in Riverside Cemetery. The monument above his resting place bears the likeness of his bronze medal, set in the Olympic rings, along with the words, "A Friend to All — Big T."

CHAPTER 12
A Giant Dies . . . and Remembered

"I really feel the lifestyle that Chris had to live as a professional wrestler contributed to his death," said Chuck Burling several years after Chris's death. "He was often beaten up and would have to drive all night and could only eat once a day, and I think this was all a part of everything that led to his circulation problems. Under this type of lifestyle, it's hard to keep your health.

"When Chris stopped wrestling he lost a lot of muscle tone and it progressively worked against him. His heart couldn't handle carrying all that weight around. Those last two years he really went down hill fast, but he refused to admit he was sick.

"I remember the last time I saw Chris alive. I had to ask him if everything was okay, and he said, 'I'm okay, everything is okay.' We shook hands, and although he had been ill his grip seemed to be back to normal. He simply said, 'I'll see you later, little buddy.' "

Nichols was surprised, but not shocked, by the death at age 29 of his giant star.

"He just hadn't looked good. I guess we all knew something wasn't right, and we feared the worst." said Nichols. "I think it was a feeling by society that someone that big might have difficulty. But, it was still a surprise that it came when it did."

Jim Duschen admitted he was surprised when he heard about Chris's death, although he was aware of his declining health.

"I would see him from time to time, and I could tell the difference each time. I felt the last two or three years, after he got sick in the summer of 1976 that he never fully recovered. He had a high fever, hepatitis, jaundice. He just didn't seem able to recover from it all."

There is evidence that Chris, too, was thinking about his death.

"I know he knew he was close to the end," said Huffman recalling the final times he was with Chris. "He would talk to me about what Lynne was going to do."

Chris Taylor was destined to go through life as a giant and, like nearly all giants, to end life at an age the rest of society's members would label premature.

Maybe it was left for Dan Gable, his great Olympic teammate, to provide the most fitting epitaph: "He died young, but he probably put his body through a total life at the age of 29."

Jennifer, Lynne, Sherri and Vera Taylor with Dowagiac coach during the cereminies at Dowagiac Union High School.

An athletic complex planned by Union High School is to be named for Chris, while the football field was renamed for him in 1983.

The Gentle Giant

There was no danger Chris was going to be forgotten by those whose lives he had touched. His Dowagiac friends established the Chris Taylor Memorial Wrestling Scholarship, to send kids to camps like Russ Houk's; Dowagiac Union High School changed the name of its All-Sports Award, which Chris shared with Burling as seniors, to the Chris Taylor Award.

An athletic complex planned by Union High School is to be named for Chris, while the football field was renamed for him in 1983. The Michigan State Legislature presented his parents with a special tribute to Chris, and he was voted into the National Junior College Hall of Fame.

Despite the titles, the awards and accolades, what stood out the most about Chris's life was the incredible contrast between his size and his nature. Duschen explained you actually had to stand next to him to appreciate his size... the massive arms, wrists like a stove pipe, the hugeness of the man." And yet, he was, by all accounts, so gentle.

Speaking at Dowagiac the year after Chris's death, Russ Houk presented a side of Chris few others were aware of. He told of their first meeting, when Chris was suffering from a facial infection and came to Houk for treatment. Houk was preparing to apply a medicine that had a real bite to it when Chris spoke up.

" 'Now, you be careful, because I know that hurts,' Chris said, 'and I can't stand pain.' And I sat there and thought, here's one of the greatest athletes I've ever known, a man who has tremendous strength...and it never dawned on me that he was a human being!

"Sometimes we think people who are big and strong and have all these great characteristics — that they're not human, that they don't hurt. And it struck me right there, and I had a different insight altogether...that this man felt pain just like you and I.

"And later, I found out he had compassion, just like you and I. But we overlooked that because of his size, and his stature, and the things he did.

"But he was very human. And that's one of the first things I noticed, and liked, about Chris Taylor."

Chris was a sensitive person, by all accounts. At a very early age he recognized he was different. The true story of his impact in the world rests in how he came to terms with his uniqueness, accepted it, and blessed others with his acceptance of who he was.

"He had a lot of emotions," said Huffman. "He was always afraid of hurting someone, emotionally or physically. They called him 'The Gentle Giant'. He was gentle because he was always afraid of hurting someone."

Jerry the artist.

That was his legacy; the legacy of all giants.

"He was the strongest man in the world, enormous in size," Houk told that gathering in Dowagiac. "But if I had anything that I was going to remember this man by — it would be his gentleness. He was one of the most gentle men I have ever known...a real contribution to the human race."

Burling, a friend since childhood, learned from

This portrait of Chis done by artist Jerry, hangs in Dowagiac High School.

The Gentle Giant

observing Chris what it means to be a giant in a world filled with "normal" people. He had seen his friend struggle to fit in, and then fit in magnificently, at last.

"He overcame what seemed like an endless stream of obstacles throughout his life, by using the gifts that many thought of as burdens," said Burling. "His combination of hard work and dedication brought him from a joked-about fat boy to an international hero. It allowed him to accomplish more in a short time than most can attain in a much longer lifetime."

Chris Taylor never let anyone down and all the memories, the bridge, the little blond kid at camp, the fake hotdog, the trampoline, the gold shirt; that will be shared and told and retold for a long time. Chris Taylor left a legacy and this was but a part of it.

Those who knew Chris Taylor, loved him. His heart, love and humor are the true memories. One can look up his wrestling records, but one cannot make statistics on the memory of him.

EPILOGUE

How big was Chris Taylor at various stages throughout his life? He weighed a very average seven pounds and four ounces when he was born June 13, 1950. By comparison, his daughter, Jennifer, weighed eight pounds and eight ounces when she was born twenty-five years later.

But Chris grew amazingly fast. He weighed 75 pounds at the age of five. As a freshman at Dowagiac Union High School, Chris weighed close to 280 pounds and stood six foot, two inches tall.

His senior year at Union High, as the defending state champion, Chris was close to 380 pounds.

Entering Iowa State University in the fall of 1971, he was put on the meat scale at the ISU animal laboratory, and weighed 416 pounds.

During his senior year in college, Chris moved to the 440-450 range.

Though it can't be officially documented, it is believed that Chris weighed over 500 pounds when wrestling professionally in the middle 1970s.

When measured for his Olympic clothing in 1972, Chris wore a size 58 long jacket and a size 15EEE shoe. Other measurements included a 22 inch neck, 52 inch waist and a 60 inch chest.

Some more facts about Chris:

- He was the largest athlete ever to compete in the Big Eight Conference.
- He was the largest athlete ever to compete in the NCAA Division I wrestling tournament.
- He was the largest athlete ever to compete in the Olympic Games.
- He was the largest athlete ever to compete in the Midlands Tournament, American's toughest mat meet.
- He is reputed to be one of the two heaviest men to ever wrestle professionally (Andre the Giant being the other).
- At 450 pounds, he was nearly 130 pounds bigger than William "The Refrigerator" Perry, who caused a media sensation while playing football for the Chicago Bears in the 1980's.
- At 450 pounds, he was heavier than five Olga Korbuts, the pixieish Soviet Union gymnast who starred in the 1972 Olympics and weighed only 87 pounds.

- At 450 pounds, he weighed as much as three Dan Gables when Gable won the 149.5 gold medal in the 1972 Olympics.
- At 450 pounds, he was twice as heavy as Muhammad Ali, world heavyweight boxing champion in the early 1970's.

The following poem was written in longhand in one of Chris's personal scrapbooks. His wife, Lynne, said he read it often and it exemplified his attitude about life. Its origin is unknown:

"When you rule the battle, look out upon the field with power in
your battle axe and victory on your shield.

"Don't breathe it in too deeply, don't let it sink too far; don't build
your future on it, whoever you are;

"For you'll hear a louder cheering when in your final fling you fade
into the shadows before the new crown came.

"So let this thought in passing sink deeply in your soul —
the fun is in the battle but seldom in the goal.

"And when the way seems easy put this down for a bit — the prize
is in the battle and you'll pay for what you get.

"So gaze upon the skyline when training for the day...
a better man than you is always on the way!"

The Gentle Giant

Chris Taylor
1950-1979